PARIS:
GENESIS OF A MUSE

JEAN-YVES VINCENT SOLINGA

FIRST EDITION

Little Red Tree Publishing, LLC,
509 W 3rd Street, North Platte, NE 69101

Previous works published with
Little Red Tree Publishing:

Clair-Obscur of the Soul (2008)
Clair-obscur de l'âme [in French] (2008)
In the Shade of a Flower (2009)
Landscape of Envies (2010)
Words Made of Silk (2011)
Impressions of Reality (2013)
Artist in a Pixelated World (2014)
Asymptotes at the Infinity of Passion:
The Untouchable Quest of Poetry (2015)
Created Realities (2017)

Layout and Cover Design: Michael Linnard, MCSD
Times New Roman, Trajan Pro and Ariel.

First Edition, 2019, manufactured in USA
1 2 3 4 5 6 7 8 9 10 LSI 25 24 23 22 21 20 19

Front cover photograph of Sacré Coeur in the distance after September hailstorm. Courtesy of Jean-Yves Solinga (the view is roughly that of the glance by Paul in *Last Tango in Paris*).

Library of Congress Cataloging-in-Publication Data

Solinga, Jean-Yves Vincent
 Paris: Genesis of a Muse/ Jean-Yves Vincent Solinga. -- 1st ed.
   p. cm.
 Includes index.
 ISBN 978-1-935656-59-3 (pbk. : alk. paper)
 I. Title.
 PS3612.A58565S77 2019
 811'.6--dc23

Little Red Tree Publishing LLC
509 W 3rd Street,
North Platte, NE 69101
www.littleredtree.com

CONTENTS

« La poésie n'a pas d'autre but qu'elle-même »
"Poetry has no other goal than itself"

« Le poète jouit de cet incomparable privilège,
qu'il peut à sa guise être lui-même et autrui. »
*"The poet enjoys the incomparable privilege of
being, as he wills, himself and someone else."*

Charles Baudelaire, « le Spleen de Paris »

FOREWORD

Here again I sit before my computer to write a foreword for another outstanding book of poems from Jean-Yves.

This is the tenth book of lyrical poetry that Little Red Tree Publishing has published in as many years. In this book Jean-Yves has taken the opportunity to tentatively explore the subject of the genesis of his own muse. The title, *Paris: Genesis of a Muse*, is therefore both a literal and a provocative ghost, in so many ways. So we are left searching for a response to the intriguing question: Who or What is this muse, or more specifically how Paris became the genesis...?

Regrettably you will find no direct or complete answer to the "genesis" or the "muse," because a description sufficient to encapsulate the infinite possibilities is by its very nature ineffable. Interestingly Jean-Yves was not born in Paris —or France—in fact has never lived for any extended period in the City. He was actually born in Algeria and moved to Morocco as a young boy where he spent an idyllic childhood and at 14 was abruptly sent to America by his family. Following an honorably discharge from the US Army he became a teacher. He gained a Masters and PhD along the way and spent his entire career teaching French Culture and Literature in Connecticut schools and colleges.

Alternatively, close examination of the front cover photograph, a typical cityscape of Paris, renders minimal clues except for the hardly discernible glimpse of the Sacré-Cœur Basilica, over the rooftops, in the distance. However, this is important. Now here the reader would be forgiven for not knowing that this photo was taken from the seventh floor of a nameless hotel. In fact a similar view that Paul, the character Marlon Brando played in *Last Tango in Paris*, gazed from. Therefore you might summise that it is the character's thoughts or feelings that are important or the sight of the magestic building and all that it represents to Parisians or in fact to the French people, even Jean-Yves himself? The Basilica is built on the highest point in Paris so it can be seen from virtually any vantage point in Paris. Is it the fact that the Catholic Basilica was commissioned aside from the obvious "glory of God," as penance for the defeat in the Franco-Prussian

War (1870), and the excesses of the socialist Paris Commune debacle of (1871)? Maybe....

Having been born outside of France with a soul that is as one with the desert (Maghreb) of North West Africa, Jean-Yves is also magnetically drawn to the epicenter of French culture and the density of its history. To be inextricably linked but essentially an observer might be the genesis, whether this is the thought or the physical touch of grains of sand passing through young fingers, or the thought of the profound secular world of Moulin Rouge at the bottom of the Montmartre hill so close to the Catholic Basilica, or indeed the flawed but still compelling pastiche of Parisian life and French Morocco, or the existentialist vision of Sartre's concept of the absurdity, where exquisite beauty exists in the same space and time as unspeakable disaster... And, one cannot wander too far from the influence of Camus, which invades the very essence of Jean-Yves.

Having said all that you might expect the book to contain a collection of poems about Paris. Regrettably you will find few directly about Paris, but all paths to find the "muse" inexibly lead back to Paris, or the thought of Paris throughout his books.

To reiterate, from many of the forewords I have written for the 10 books, Jean-Yves is a prolific writer... I continue to be in awe of his ability.

Michael Linnard,
North Platte, NE, 2019

ACKNOWLEDGEMENT

I deeply appreciate the continuing support and friendship of Michael Linnard. Small publishing houses like Little Red Tree are part of the critical network that writers have always needed over the years: No less than Marcel Proust, among too many others, had at first been refused publication.

I would like to mention a warm place in my heart for the following: the memory of my father, Marcel Laurent Solinga, mother, Anna Félicie Ciccariello Solinga, and my brother, Pierre Paul.

To my sister Marie Louise Menders. My children Robert Marcel, his wife Elizabeth and son Luc. My daughter Nicole Anne and husband Marc Stasi, their children Noëlle and Luciana.

To the splendid souls, on three continents, who have filled my life since youth and who have had a role in defining the singularity in the various "visages" of happiness.

And a particularly special appreciation for my wife Elaine, who has nobly accepted my hours on the computer with unwavering loving support.

Jean-Yves Vincent Solinga
March 2019

On the Seine, facing Notre Dame de Paris.
Photo by Elaine Solinga.

PREFACE

The following lines are from the correspondence between Albert Camus and Maria Casarès: Letters that J.-P. Enthoven qualified as between "sensual and sparkling pagans."

In one of his earliest letters, dated June 1944, at one in the morning, Albert Camus writes:

"Bonne nuit, mon chéri. Que demain vienne vite et les autres jours où tu seras plus à moi qu'à cette maudite pièce. Je t'embrasse de toutes mes forces. AC."

"Good night, my darling [nota bene: Camus uses the masculine regarding Maria, as a form of endearment]. May tomorrow arrive quickly and the other days when you will be more mine than to this damn play. I kiss you with all my strength."

Touching dichotomy of sentiments, from one of the greatest philosophers of the twentieth century: Albert Camus. On one hand, at ease dealing with cosmological questions for mankind, in an absurd world; with no absolutes as references... yet at a loss, alone in his room, desperate like a lovelorn teenager for morning light, to find his lover Maria Casarès.

This superb contradiction in our human nature is what continues to drive my poetry.

Titles like "Dying Ripples" or "Like Job" may give the impression of a tone of retrospective or submission to the passage of time in this collection of poems. But a line from one of my earliest poems, is still relevant to what has always been my state of mind when writing: Written, first in French, it is simply: *"On perd la jeunesse... mais on garde la passion."* "We lose youth... but keep the passion."

I continue to have this view of *life and living* by grounding my ideas in a secular awe of our awareness of existence. It gives the artist the spectacular opportunity to *glorify one's past... for having lived it.*

And so... yes... some poems do deal with the ugliness of societies, with the effects of war on children ("Sea Urchins"); but it is more often the nobility of human resilience that I emphasize. Such as the lack of basic food for the supper table and yet... the gathering of these shellfish on the rocks, yards away from marauding Nazi guards. Such human resistance, mental and physical, defines—for me—human solidarity at its most natural state.

Thus, some poems make use of historic events: some from close-up, as witnessed and retold by family members or extended circles of acquaintances. However, they are all reconstituted in term of linearity and characters: events and people have been transferred. ("Return from Viet Nam," "Hollow Parade," "Lush Green Fields," among others.)

Other poems are pure fantasies (sometimes headed by the telling subtitle, "A Fable:") built however, on a real infrastructure. But, at no time, is my work an attempt at *authoritative or exact personal nonfiction*: Victor Hugo did a lot of research for *Les misérables*, but a doctoral thesis adviser would frown on a dissertation on the French penal system solely based of this novel.

Therefore, as a work of fiction, I reserve the exhilarating freedom of "making stuff up" and fill the interspaces with as much reality as needed.

This guiding principle applies for the building blocks of personae in the poems. The best compliment made to a writer of fiction has to be: "She seems so real! She could be someone I even know!" Well it may well be... but, in my poem, she may well be made up of three persons from three different continents.

As usual, I have added embellishments, pastiches, and disregard for a timeline to give me the freedom of creating my own world and personalities. In writing "Tralfamadorian Man," the mind, vision, and modus operandi of Kurt Vonnegut, helped me reach escape velocity from some of the constraints of linear topics and people in our lives. For instance, the re-appearance of the character of *Sidi Moussa* (see notes) and the North African world, are bits and pieces of a world long gone but still rich in teaching moments and rites of passage for me. So, it is, that the seamless mix of fiction and reality, sought by such as a Kurt Vonnegut, adds the ultimate creative dimension of "flexible time." Writing "Tralfamadorian Man" was like being on a train and looking up with astonishment at the name of the next station. The incestuous and arbitrary of time, place, and people were absolutely liberating.

Viet Nam (directly and indirectly) makes a return in this book. It is the result of a long, "Cognac driven" discussion about the byzantine determination of "1A and deferment draft status." Wars kill soldiers and civilians: it is the survivors who must continue with the memories and poems... like "Flanders Fields."

Paris, as the title states, continues to take up a lot of space in my heart: The city has had the unusual role of *inspiring and breaking* it. "May '68," the room on the "seventh floor" and the very polite French answer from the person behind the ticket window: "Non... Monsieur... je m'excuse... les trains sont en grève." ["No... Sir... I apologize... the trains are on strike."]

Or the difficult… Hollywood-like separations at the airport, where I see Paris, playing the role of a Greek chorus in a tragedy.

Sometimes a poem offers itself upon walking into *that hotel room*, as in poem "Paris: Genesis of a muse": A moment that feels like a director finding the exact location for a camera angle: "That's the view from 'Last Tango'…!" I just knew it. I could feel Marlon Brando in the room with me.

Albert Camus represents and also brings out complicated sentiments in me. This elegant philosopher came down from the tower, usually associated with writers, to deal with, or is it… to impale himself, on… problems found in the gooey ink of newspapers headlines: In particular the French war in Algeria. Cosmological thoughts rarely come out unscathed from writing about military uprisings and police roundups. Camus is no exception.

Jean-Yves, circa, 1949, in Salé, Morocco, across from the khasbah of the Chellah.

But Camus's love for North Africa parallels mine. It is an honest love, for a complicated land, and neither one of us needs to feel ashamed of our "foreign" presence. My attraction to the land, as a teenager, was akin to any "object of desire" [the sun, the landscape, the majestic date trees, the huge mud walls of the Udayas Kasbah, across the street]. The deep blue Mediterranean Sea is not conscious of real-politick.

For this reason, the poem "High on a cliff in North Africa" sets itself apart: It is about two important topics and themes prevalent in my poetry; Albert Camus and the North African imagery.

The formers were both important subjects of my doctoral thesis [*Evolution et constantes: représentation(s) du site maghrébin chez Loti, Gide, Camus et Le Clézio.*] [Evolution and Stasis: Representation(s) of the Maghreb in the Works of Loti, Gide, Camus, and Le Clézio]. Although the abstract states that the thesis is an analysis of the description, tools, and roles of the Maghrebian landscape in these authors, the attributes of this physical world is seen, purposefully, through "a non-denominational, non-religious lens."

I explained, in my doctoral introduction, that my work was strictly non-sociological and non-political. I wanted to present this landscape through secular eyes. It was a position that did not go without notice [and criticism]: "How can you suggest that you… an outside observer [the Other], not feel obligated to take into account the very status of [your or these writers'] French colonial nature."

My answer then, and now, is that the "human passion" for the emptiness of the land, the solar silence, the solidity of the heat... the whiteness of the sun are based in the universal ingredient of the absolute neutrality of the physical world in things religious. The universe and therefore the landscape in Camus' world and mine are not predicated on a divinity. The gods mentioned are simply useful literary descriptors from learned studies. The landscape at Tipaza remains (in my mind, at least) secular. Previous and subsequent societies, having introduced religion(s) as they wished.

My love for the Maghreb—and I suggest Camus' also—is from the same cloth as the love one has from seeing one's mother's face. It is simply there. Robert Frost's love and appreciation for the beauty of a New England winter should not need to add a disclaimer for his immigrant/invader ancestors to the New World in order to glorify the crystalline blue of winter skies. Karen Blixen's love for the land in "Out of Africa" and other Anglophone artists come to mind as well.

My style, the structural rules of my poetry tend towards the "lyrical prose": At times like the "poetic-prose" of my early French readings; such writers as Baudelaire [poêmes en prose] or the lyrical prose of Camus in his first "carnets" [notebooks] (such as "Tipaza:, "l'Été," and Le Clézio [especially in "Désert"]).

Jean-Yves Vincent Solinga
Gales Ferry, Connecticut 2019

PARIS:
GENESIS OF A MUSE

Paris: Genesis of a Muse

Dedicated to those who have known the congruences of the heart, places, and emotional disponibility* that manifest themselves, during privileged moments.

"We'll always have Paris,"
Kept playing in his mind. In this bed. In a hotel's seventh floor.
The setting, so authentic that a World War II Nazi occupation film
had required only a few "modern" pieces to be removed.

From the tortuous rue Saint Lazare, that righteously crosses rue des Martyrs,
you walked directly into authentic history:
going through a four-inch wooden door
that had probably seen the blood smears of revolutions
and glorious tears of heartbreaks.

But instead, his mind jumped to the artifice of Hollywood:
"We'll always have Paris."

The craving for his own need to recreate this city:
miraculously, turning the celluloid world of *Casablanca*,
into the seminal soup of artificial reality.

———————————————————

"We'll always have Paris,"
was more akin to an act of faith:
a credo to be accepted in one's heart of heart.

These words… from a mundane movie-script, meant to him,
that only disciples of the magic of memories
could really sit at the table.

Casablanca, the movie, had nothing in common with realism.
The people, the bar, the street scenes.
He knew that. He had lived there.

The clothing looked more like a New York interpretation
of the Moroccan world.

A commedia dell'arte:
where actors served a faithful representation of their character's identity:

The Nazis: nauseously brutal.
The black-marketers: perfectly neutral.
The flawed protagonist: refusing to do the wrong thing.
And the heroine's honor: like a priceless Limoges porcelain.

"And yet... it worked!" he murmured, upon reflecting on the movie.
Casablanca had captured the ingredients of memories.

For, in spite of all the easy imitations of Bogart's lines
And the low elevation of production,
The couple's quiet, delusional *passion of return,*
sounds so true after all these years.

"Mankind has been *saddled* with the capacity to recall the past," he
would complain.
Having already attempted a visceral voyage
back to the solar warmth of his Promise Land.
To Sidi Moussa:
That magical beach on the tip of Africa;
And at the center of his soul.

Sidi Moussa... like Paris... still intact in their artistic cocoon.
Untouched and unspoiled by the vagaries of time.
Still proudly exhibiting its engorged red prickly pears,
in the dryness of spotless blue skies:
in the iodized spray of the green Atlantic.

Sidi Moussa, prophet... his patron-saint of the illuminated;
of the deluded urban and desert traveler.
The saintly figure who now, guides lovers to the Pont Neuf:
Not far from the kisses, sighs... and oaths
of nihilists and atheists.

Now...
lying passively in this humble room, overlooking Paris.
Feeling embarrassedly envious of the ease provided, by their
Religious zeal, to these figures of history and religious texts:
"Moses: so sure, of himself. So sure, of a hands-on god.
Such unquestioned exaltation!":
He thought to himself!

She was at the window when he awoke.

A translucent overlay,
of her porcelain-white nudity under a nightgown.

Her curves acting like a découpage tracing
over the foggy, grayish-whiteness of le Sacré Coeur.

She whispered, as though to a presence on the balcony:
"C'est beau... hein?
Oui... toujours. Même sous la pluie.
Surtout sous la pluie." He added:

As if echoing Verlaine,
whose stanzas on Paris they would recite to each other.

All the while, the virginal shades of the Basilica gave a shawl of modesty
to the carnal world on the Place Blanche and Moulin Rouge, at its feet.

In Paris, the emanations of human passions
—their attractions and their repulsions—
Making you acquire the natural feel of a second skin.

They incrust themselves
into the very substance of walls and cobblestones of the city.

He remembered, trying in his youth, to pry out, to capture
—in the after lunch walk to school—
all... the vastness of the Maghrebian nothingness.

How could the bleds** be so empty and yet alive?
How could these dead Roman cities still contain urban noise?
Why did the stones of the highways of the Roman empire, insist on
retaining the grooves of the cartwheels?
Remembering the words of André Gide that:

"Sight was the most frustrating of the senses."
He confronted the oppressive silence
and ambivalent grainy horizon of the Sahel.

And here he is now... in the Parisian mist:
Understanding the nature of her tears:

She knew...
for having been his muse all these years...
she knew... what he felt as he looked at her.

She knew... on this balcony and this backdrop,
that multitude of tableaux were lining up.

She knew...
of his pilgrimages to stand in silent reverence in museums.

She knew...
he could hear his own words:
—an inner voice for such moments of happiness—

"That one should die, when one is so happy."
Having no more to live for.
"Where art decodes reality":
He once said, in front of a Jacques-Louis David.

A confirmed non-believer,
he felt himself watched by secular, mundane, jealous gods.

Gods, somehow envious of the human happiness
That can somehow survive in pockets of mankind.

A concept... a scene, set in Paris by Henry Miller,
would, then invade him, when in full earthy euphoria.

Miller's narrator is in bed with two women,
expecting, at any moment, the door to be swung wide-open
by an enraged, jealous, random passer-by from the street below!

Paris... that Paris!
A place that makes you a voyeur
of your own voyeurism.

A random cosmic intersection
containing all *earthy nourishments* that one would ever need.

Paris... not a place; but a state of mind.
A location, on the third rock from the sun,
that would eventually grow life equipped with self-reflection.

"And one of them would be... *me!*"
He murmured, looking at her at the window.

Paris had acquired the power to transcend time and space:
Requiring personal disponibility* and a synesthesia of the senses.

It would happen between the viewer
and the painted vocabulary on the museum walls.

A place that —like for Dorothy toward Kansas—
Would have to wish upon... three times:
"We'll always have Paris"
... To make it so.

The balcony. The view of Montmartre.
He was becoming a doppelganger of the Marlo Brando character:
he was reliving the last scene of "Last Tango in Paris."

He had brought her to this city in spite of and because of... all conventions:
Like some perverted classroom practicum, for both of them.

Everything existed at once:
Dichotomy. Overstimulation of the senses. Emptiness of the soul.
Her unfathomable youth, reminding him of another one.

One of the sexually dissipated youth found in *Rolla:*
with its duality of debauchery and New Testament virginity.

The nihilism in passages he had discussed in his courses:
Meursault and Brando's character, practically dead soul at the start:

"I… so much wanted to enter their world… their lives:
Slap their faces and tell them:
Wake up! Down by the Opéra… on the bridges,
you can still hear the whispers of past lovers… by lovers repeated.

The contrast of the organic remnants of hedonism all around.
And then… this camera close-up.

There is a childlike sadness, in Paul's glance,
as he looks upon toward *what will continue to exist*
—after his imminent death—
on top of Montmartre.

And all… he wanted to do now,
was to jump out of bed and cover her with a blanket,
in order to shield her body
from divine lust!

In homage to Charles Baudelaire's Paris and his "prose poétique."
See the Glossary for a definition of "Disponibility."
**Moroccan for "countryside."*

Dying Ripples

Like Moses in his desert…
He… also was offered a morsel of happiness:
This time, by Her… his true divinity.

He refused.

Going back, instead, to die a solitary death, in the emotional wilderness.

He did not
—even with this *divine* dispensation—
Deign to glimpse, once more, on the *Promised land*:

Her eyes.

He would rather spend the rest of his days
Reconstructing floral perfumes of anticipated next minutes.
Or, willing glances, perceived in the shadows.

In spite of the visceral pain… he would rather labor at his art:
Recreating cherished intrusions from the past.
Incongruous pastel-apparitions in the sterility of business meetings,

That left his soul whispering: "She had the same hair style."

Her fondness for cumin, eliciting the Maghrebian heat
found in cheap Parisian couscous:
Prelude to bohemian hours of hedonism in a seventh-floor walk-up:

Trembling mirages over a Mediterranean beach.
The psychological synesthesia of her black bikini-clad flesh,
Incestuously linked to scents of her favorite solar cream.

He had learned to live in the safety of an *acquired* past.
Somehow finding the strength to reply:
"… the price of holding you *temporarily* is too great."

Circumstances would allow ex-lovers to be together one last time: He refused.

The Burial Suit of an Immigrant

It was not the seemingly-far-away echo in the surgeon's voice;
And the deadly nature of the adjectives used.

It was not the ominous buzzing of the hallway neon lights,
Acting their part in the tragedy.

Nor the silent ride home in a taxi:
Past the bridge, his father would never see again.

Not even the dignified privacy
Of the mother's muffled cry in the bathroom.

It happened... rather...
After the last of the family had gently closed the door:
Its sticky handle still exhibiting its triumphal recalcitrance
to the father's repairs.

It came almost as a surprise:
A heartbreaking question, inserted in the day's pain.
An unexpected touching comment on the true nature of the day:
The sublime born from the mundane:

She would have her husband buried in his work clothes:
The ones of his new persona in the New World.

The ones, with the stubborn stains of menial status he wore,
with the same pride as a Spahis, in his youth:
"Will you have your father's work clothes dry-cleaned?"

A wife's recognition of her husband's immigrant status by having his stained and ripped work clothes meticulously dry cleaned for his burial.

Nuit de Chine

Rabat, Morocco (circa 1953)

Multi-layered apprehension and confusion,
Upon entry into this sacristy of sensualities.

Private boudoir of secretive grande-dame,
With arrangement of relics of a convoluted past.
A holy of holies of sights… touch and especially… smells.

It would be, before its full understanding, an introduction
to the symbiotic soup
made of the irresistibility of sin and the purity of idealism:

Our nonjudgmental disponibility* to human attractions:
The immediacy of youthful icons that pass them as happiness.

Such as this ageless woman:
statuesque demeanor with impeccable speech intonations.

Oasis… in this solar world
exquisite gâteaux de soirée and Limoges flutes
On traditional copper trays with hand-hammered arabesques.

A feminine presence in black Chanel silk
Contrasting against white marbly skin:
Separating her from any ties to reality.

Everything of this exotic world… has disappeared:
save my mother's blue eyes, across on the sanguine love seat
and my presence on a lazy pouf full of leathery smells.
And… from the dressing table
the ever-present whiffs of Nuit de Chine.

Everything in this room… it turned out… would evolve
into other icons of the precious and everlasting… in the human soul.

Our knowing recognition of what is eternal
in the ephemeral language of things.
And an apparent correct interpretation, as a little boy,
Of the vaporous truths in this flask of petal-oils.

Deep impressions, upon a little boy, by visits in the "boudoir" of an enigmatic family friend.
*See the Glossary for a definition of "Disponibility."

Pastis on the Patio

A quirky personal and joyfully cultural way
Of showing one's disdain of time and place:
A first seasonal drink on the patio.

Seasonal ritual of human imposition on things:
A glorious pastis… alcoholic infusion of aromas of Provence.

Time and memories…
captured in a Proustian synesthesia of milky clouds.

Verandas overlooking pine-scented hills;
Shy cicadas singing the heat of the day,
Like hedonistic Titans,
seemingly getting their energy from the sun's rays;

All these visions…
in the green puritanism of New England's snowy memories.

Cooling swims at the Pointe Rouge.
An athletic father's finely muscular back, as my boat.

Mixture of eternity and moment.
And hoping for both.

The razor-edged balance of Mediterranean joys and sorrows:
But for a glance at the neighbors' yard,

And its thriving grass… since his death.

A gentle reminder from the universe of our intrusion… in it.

Voir sous les jupes

Visions et impulsions sensuelles de jeunesse:
Dans cet espace mystérieux.

Région apparemment protégée et isolée,
projetant sa propre chaleur visuelle.

Monde fait de pastels lisses,
moulant des chairs vallonnées et cachées:

Se voulant timides
et pourtant si riches en symboles futurs.

Premiers frissons de contradiction :
Entre la vue et la possession.

Le besoin et l'esquisse d'une soif.
Le monde et ses limites.

L'innocence naturelle de la curiosité du regard.
Et l'omniprésence réprobatrice maternelle.

Genèse de l'existence des fruits défendus
qui divisent la simplicité du touché et le poids de la signification.

Tourbillons et contrastes de couleurs.
Arabesques serpentines de tissus imprimées.
Blanc cru et sévère de coton.

Souvenirs d'enfance : école primaire mixte après l'école de garçons. Cour de récréation et coup d'œil accidentel sous les jupes des petites camarades de classe.

Looking Under Skirts

Visions and youthful sensual impulses,
unto this mysterious space.

Apparently protected and isolated region,
projecting its own visual heat.

World made of smooth pastels,
molding waves of hidden flesh.

Proclaiming timidity
and yet so rich in future symbols.

First contradictory shivers,
between sight and possession.

Need and drink.
The world and its limits.

The natural innocence of the inquiring glance.
And the omnipresence of the stern maternal eyes.

Genesis of the existence of forbidden fruits,
which divide the simplicity of the touch and the weight of its meaning.

Swirls and contrasting colors.
Snaking arabesques of printed fabric.
Strident and severe white of the cotton.

Youthful memories: mixed-gender primary school-yard playtime, after all-boys establishment, and the accidental "under the skirts" view of girl schoolmates.

The First Second

Sleepwalking trek, during a deep New England winter.
The topic of the up-coming lecture:
The concept of some *divine direction* in mankind's condition...
...and... more immediately for the student:
how to keep his toes from freezing in the next minutes.

The *very existence* of time
—according to the student in back of the smallish lecture hall—
inherent from the decomposition of matter
begun from its inception in the Big Bang... or any previous ones.

"Why should Time exist and why should it go forward...
in that decomposition?"

The existential importance
of the very *existence of a second*... of the first second!

And the afore-mentioned "troublemaker"
from the cheap seats adding:

"I'm a complete atheist... I couldn't care less about God or gods.
Not anti... simply not interested."

A frostbite on the horizon... the eerie stillness of Nature,
somehow producing a sharper focus:

The placid frozen whiteness, and just...
a university-trained mind,
pondering on *this forward movement*
toward his old age... or the start of the lecture.

Memories of early morning university philosophy class (circa 1960's)

Sanctum Sanctorum

Refaire Paris

Que les notes glissent gentiment en perles
de douceur sur ses muscles tendus:
Titillation de la main droite et soupirs des touches blanches.

Palpitation de la gauche… sans pitié.
Plutôt revigorée par les murmures de douleur du frottement.

Splendide manifestation d'abandonnement aux rites de l'extase.
Échos de tous les coins de la chambre assombrie, retenus par l'intimité de
leur univers.

Grimace de son regard dominant acquiesçant,
aperçu à travers le désordre noir emmêlé d'une forêt d'hédonisme,

Se mêlant au sien perplexe,
Dans une trouée s'ouvrant sur un spectaculaire carmin ;

Et… à une prise de conscience :
Que les dieux—en se trompant—devaient l'avoir curieusement choisi
Pour une rare et frustrante dégustation d'une vision féminine :
Au centre, le plus chéri, de leurs privilèges égoïstes.

English version first published as "Inner Sanctum, Reconstructing Paris," in *Asymptotes at the Limit of Passion* (2015.)

Inner Sanctum

Reconstructing Paris

Let the notes gently glide in beads
of softness over her taut muscles:
Titillating right hand and sighs from the white keys.

Pulsating left… with no pity:

Rather invigorated by the gentle whimpered pain of friction.
Splendid display of abandonment to the rites of ecstasy.

Echoes from all the corners of the darkened room kept within their
intimate universe.

Her grimacing dominating glance of approval, looking regally down
Through a black tangled forest of hedonism,

Linking to his own bewildered one
And a widening opening unto a spectacular crimson,

Leading to his realization
That the gods must have somehow mistakenly chosen him

For a rare taste and frustrating feminine glimpse
Into their most cherished selfish privileges.

To the music of TAO Lounge 4 "In the mood" by Monte la rue. First published in French
in *Asymptotes at the Infinity of Passion* (2015).

Philosophy At the Town Dump

Succinct abstract,
of Kant's definition of human consciousness,
witnessed in this "run to the dump":

Discreet building on the far side.
Cacophony of dog-barking in multiple octaves.

"Last stop. Last chance" according to the attendant:
"This last batch doesn't have much hope for a reprieve!"

Betraying an emotional breaking of his voice
in this huge dog-pound keeper.

"Not a chance! … all runts!"
"Nobody wants them!"

Ah! The power of fictionalized reality
The hilarious Peggy Lee-scene of the "Lady and the tramp,"
Filtered out the reciprocal heartbreaking sadness
Between the dogs and the omnipotence of a cartoonist.

Surprisingly philosophical statement from the town dump/dog pound attendant, on an appropriately rainy morning: "These creatures do not know how little they have to live."

How Did It Feel?

Chemin du Roucas Blanc, Marseille (last days of World War Two): where ten local residents coming back from work by tramway, were randomly lined up and shot as reprisal for the underground's killing of a German officer.

How did it feel
when you heard the release of the rope?
That instant before the cold blade cut through you neck?

Did aristocratic visions
of the genesis of this moment flow by your conscience?

The latest pastries from Paris and Vienna?
What of your husband?
Or unaccounted fortune spent on your grand-father's palace?
Bankruptcies of the heart and ethics

———————————

What of the Roman senators, a few centuries before,
hearing the guttural roar of the Vandals going up the marble steps?

Did you have gulps of pity for your wife and mistress,
as your civilization was going to be raped—stone by beautiful stone—
by envious onlookers from the North?

———————————

All these injustices of societies and cultures;
ignored through the opiate of debauched selfishness.

Confusing the attractions of refinement with those of cruelty.

———————————

What of the wordless surprise,
from the proud Indian tribe leader, in his best attire,
Feeling the hot metal lead-shot in his neck
from these strangely clothed men:
On the banks of the Mystic river?

When did it become evident to the captain of the slave ship,
—smoking his afternoon pipe on the upper deck—

that the rebellious humanity in the bowels of the ship
had mirrors for eyes?

And that their fate was his?

Did the Gestapo soldier see a piece of himself in the eyes
Of the men up against the granite wall?

How did it feel?

Hollow Parade

"You know... which kid I'm talking about. The one from "the project.
The one who was not in our "college prep" classes.
Took a different bus to his side of town.
You know: never ran for office.
Well... I read that he was one of the first from our high school class to die in Viet Nam."

Kid from the project...
pejorative loosely hurled to indict the parents' wallet.

Skin tint with a hint
of the seed of this country's original sin.

The left-overs
of miscegenation and the plantation owner's egalitarian lust.

Kid from the project...
or so it was indicated in the Other's glance.

The one...
from the flimsily-built surplus houses.

The ones
with compressed cardboard walls
and sprinkling of horse-hair substance in between.

World war two houses.
That war of existentialist threat to Uncle Sam.

Kid from the project...
one of the first to die... while last in line for the good seats.

Double troubling vision,
of his black skin and so beautiful, easy smile.

Asked in turn... like his grandfather, on Omaha Beach,
to once again rise and defend, as a good tenant,
his part of ownership of this land.

Now slated to stand for grandiose crystalline ideals:
sprinkled into the pregnant humid clouds over jungles.

One of the first to die
to defend very personal democratic goals:
somehow attached to impersonal worlds.

Kid from the project,
now introduced to grandiose geo-political equation
—with multi-unknowns—
sleeps in the eternity of his mother's tears.

To the sound of hollow yearly parades...
of quaint fire trucks,
In quaint historic New England village.

Elephant Cemetery

"The horror… the horror!" *

Cavernous voice-over sound track
about the ravages of psychotic wars and meltdowns of civilizations.

Heart wrenching nihilism
and flat-toned sadness of a fictional war hero:
himself, one of its own worst instigators:
Now having gone *primitive nativism.*

Or… what of the judgmental disdain of a father, **
gently cradling his Super-son
—as he challenges an entire planet—
for its ignorance of an existential danger?

Hollywood's unparalleled, fictionalized entertainment pulp remains,
unfortunately…
our better conveyer of wisdom for the masses.

As we collectively fail to connect, to our own image,
the one of this dusty cemetery.

Real horror of dead or dying elephants in Africa, victims of poaching, climate change and human overpopulation encroachment, as statements of our future.
* Last words of the crazed protagonist in "Apocalypse Now."
** Jor-El, as superman's father.

Back From Viet Nam *

Can't stand it no more
The people dying
Crying for help for so many years
But nobody hears
Better end soon my friend
It better end soon my friend
Can't take it no more
The people hating
Hurting their brothers
They don't understand
They can't understand
Better end soon my friend
(Chicago "It Better End Soon")

On the sink... **

All she said was: "Hello."
In retrospect, that is all *youth*... needs.

Strangely sounding... years later...
how such innocuous phrases could attract shreds of happiness.

Or, at least, what made the *accidental*
feel like a soothing balm on an oozing scar.

We seemed to receive energy from such things:
Compounding tomorrows with it.

A bottle of beer, shared with
otherwise very sedate professional friends.

Transported into a market place
of emotional adventure.

Tasteless 60's beer, acting like a medieval elixir:
Turning the room into a merry-go-round of centrifugal attractions.

A million emotional-miles removed
from accounting for military issued M-16 rifles.
To *temporary* owner.

"It'd better end soon..."
The stereo: trying to keep up with the voice of survivor-guilt
and the noise of the clueless crowd in the living room...
but nobody is listening...
not then... not now.

She... had a deep voice
which seemed made of the waves on the moon-lit reeds on the marsh.

A faceless sound
whose glance he had yet to meet.

Then the eyes!
Especially the eyes... over his shoulder.

His craving miraculously answered by the perfect match
—After all these months of pure brutal testosterone—
by a feminine virility, attached to an intelligent sensuality.

Ah! To be blessed with redemptive moments like this!
Moments, that divide one's life like the pages of mankind:

Time for deaths.
Time for resurrections.
Time for happier endings.

Lives and souls divided in messianic ways,
In the hippish fog of incense.

Moments that turn our bodies around:
From organized brutality to gentle abandonment.

To see something for the first time.
That look... over the shoulder.

Moments in life that define pointedly
some sort of preparation for the rest of it.

......He had received his draft notice, on the way to his Calvary:
Having left a good part of his vital energy on the floor
of a hospital room along with his religious beliefs.

His father dead among the white sheets,
with a young priest offering perspectives.

Oaths were made to the silent bed room walls
to not allow himself or others to be hurt by love again.
Never more.

Away from war.
Feeling safe on this sink.
First party on first job.

A quick look around over the crowd.
A slight boozy haze giving enough distance for not getting involved.

Heated conversations about the "number of cylinders"
and the "inappropriate behavior of roommates."

The kind of solid, practical anxiety
that pulls you back into the mud of daily life.

It makes it such... that you cannot fly over it
and thus, wonder what the rest of the topography will look like.
Not allowing you a look into the future.

Huge... big brown eyes...
All she said was: "Hello"
and another part of life was off and running.... .

* Fictionalized reconstruction from real events and persons. (see introduction)
** "On the sink" ...Perfect perch, for the small statured-protagonist in the poem to be
eye-to-eye in this party, in overcrowded kitchen.

Lush-Green Fields

Reconstruction of a Viet Nam war veteran.

Her name meant "Flower of Paradise."
Still folded,
in the elegance of her native calligraphy:
inside his DD214.

Had he been trying to keep the memories safe?
Or keeping them from escaping into his present?

"...If ye break faith with us who die
We shall not sleep, though poppies grow
*In Flanders fields..." ... ***
These lines kept running in his mind,
as he first set foot on these lush-green, killing fields.

Pliable curvatures of tropical gentleness;
Violated by the brutality of dehumanization
that had been invaded from helicopters above the paddies.

He never was able to stop wondering, if, indeed,
"… poppies would, one day, re-flower this jungle."

All the while,
remaining shreds of his ethics could only hope that
She might have added to the beauty of this world:

"The way the poppies had done…
in Flanders Fields…
among the dead".

"In Flanders fields" (John McCrae, 1872-1918)

Repeated History

"Full Metal Jacket" (revisited)

The ultimate respect,
to the torn remains of the "kid from New England."
In the mannerism of La Pietà
Battle-hardened G.I.'s crying.

Glazed-eyed squad of *youngsters-soldiers* gathered around the dying
convolutions of life.
Each an icon of the dichotomy of civilization and decency amidst darkness:

Possibly, an oblique glance to the Renaissance
in the *adoration of the Christ-child.*

An attentive surrounding of
the obligatory solid presence of a long-ago disillusioned black draftee.

A border-line literate, rural, racist "good old-boy."

An aloof intellectual, whose wit has been muted by too many hosing
abdominal wounds.

The hardcore ex-gang member, now disgusted with the inescapable violence.

A panoply of actors and truths:
Mostly mundane characters and surrealistic laws,
Coming together on a devastated stage with an absentee divinity.

Late, much too late,
to impart on anyone…
the power to change:
the smell of sulfur,
rotting flesh,
and dying souls.

Liberally inspired by the squad leader's death—in the "sniper "scene—in "Full Metal Jacket": When his comrades gather around his dying body.

Blackout

"... There are moments of kindness, in horrible times, like light going apparently unimpeded through a flawless diamond, that comes out in a blinding spectrum." [unattributed member of a Cognac infused conversation]

By all accounts she was the best fed of the household:
This world war had not affected the inner mountains of the island.
Birds of the maquis thrived as well as the black-market goods.

Ration-coupons entitling the bearer to uneatable "protein" cookies.
Coffee grounds made of roasted chestnut shells and dubious pasta with assortments of mouse droppings.

Was it feline intuition... recognition for her spot next to wood-fed oven?
A privileged seat on the grandmother's blanket?

A taste of the lactose intolerant toddler's precious goat milk?
Did she read, better than some of the uncaring more fortunate neighbors,
the father's agony for not providing for his family...

... Blackout appeared on the stone ledge of the kitchen widow,
Meowing for attention of a stolen Roquefort cheese:
Still wrapped in greasy newspaper images of war propaganda.

"Blackout": Solid black-coat female cat named after the infamous "lights out" in World War II Corsica.

Sea Urchins

World War II Corsica

I can see by your coat my friend
You're from the other side
There's just one thing I got to know
Can you tell me, please, who won?
("Wooden ships," Cosby, Still, Nash & Young)

Wars…
Seven-year old little girl's world
of iodized freshness, from the North African winds.

Walks down to rocky beach
where Roman traders must have moored with amphoras full of wine.

Father's huge steady hands
opening shellfish on the beach:
His hands as steady as his transfixing military glance.

It seemed like year-long vacations.
Schools closed. Primitive freedom in post cultural apocalypse.

Echoes of kindness:
goat milk—for intolerant baby—and smuggled wild-boar sausage
from the Maquis,
miraculously appearing inside kitchen shutters.

While the mother picked greenish mold
from unidentifiable food.

———————————————————

And admits the reddish naval battle flashes in the night skies,
the precious bounty and sanguine goodness of sea-urchins.

The benevolent image of the Mediterranean Sea for an eight-year-old girl, during the food shortages in World War II, Corsica.

The Tears of Hannibal

Like an army's remains,
strewn on some battlefield:

Crushed dolls and soiled diapers;
Baby bottles and toddler's jackets;
Broken statuettes and kitchen utensils.

Pieces of the mundane,
that used to make the mundane a goal.

A defeated army, before its first battle:
without Delacroix's elephant-grandeur;
and no feats of mountain crossings.

These ragtag descendants,
driven by clouds of yellow sand,
will be another chapter in messianic travels.

But with a deceptive starlight;
and no wise men in sight.

Reflections on the migrants leaving Libya for Europe (second decade of 21th century).

The Two Faces of Joanna:

Two artists' representations of their own reality of the same model.

Lost in the meanders of the half-slumber of a morning-after:
Too much Nouvau Baujolais, too much "remaking the world,"

Too much inhalation of unfiltered Gitanes,
Along with the intoxication of *her* latest floral perfume from Grasse.
Too much.

Paris...
at the intersection and the occasional cohabitation of eternal opposites.
A place that facilitates the incestuous embrace
between the apparently virtuous and the attractively infernal.

Visions of two re-compositions of life:
In the same model; in the same city. A few years apart.
Courbet's "l'Origine du monde."
And Whistler's "Symphony in White No1."

Whistler... the extraction of the virginal covering the sexual
and then Courbet...
the quasi-pornographic revealing the innocently-natural.

Two faces of Eve... in Joanna Wiffernan:
exhibiting the splendid complexity of life.

Descending from her perch on the museum wall,
into his tired extended arms,
to then collapse on an inadequate mattress, unworthy of her receival.

"In the last room, to the right, with a view of Montmartre:"
Those fateful words from Madame la concierge,
acting the part of a Greek chorus and "House Madame."

Joanna...double-edged message of freedom and choices:
Love and cruelty.
Beauty... but its secular limits.

The moist carnal statement of her body.
And...
the blackhole pull of her glance,
within clouds of white mousseline.

He wakes up and recognizes the repurposed pre-World War II wardrobe:
A pretentious ex-estate piece
against the opposite wall from the porte-cochère window...

its full-length mirror, unconsciously reflecting the priceless presence
of the Basilica in the dying early-night photons.

The Place Blanche.
The Basilica of Montmartre.

His mind jumps once again, between the extremes:
Where artists, thinkers and lovers exist,
For having dared to live in the moment... within the moments;
and yet, still wanting to preserve it:
by wanting to know how all this works.

Wanting to take it apart with a child's careless awe:
And then... rebuild it.

Yes!... He had visited Courbet's l'Origine du Monde
He knew that it told only half the story of "life and living."

Once upon about the same time... in Paris, a few blocks from each other,
Existed this woman within two men.

She incarnated, in the mind and the art of two artists...
complementary parts that had been divided upon crossing the gates of Eden:
When the gods made us chose between flesh and soul.

Leaving to artists, to labor in the duality of existence
that make artists run to their piano and brushes, chisels and note books.

This woman representing the shimmering crimson
of life-giving flesh;
the other… in draping of white nuances, in quasi communion dress.

Seemingly… the organic attraction of the beautiful Lucifer, in one,
followed by appeasing textile shield, of the second.

Glorious symphony of the virginal and carnal of
life and living.

The two images of the same model, Joanna Hiffernan, between Courbet's "l'Origine du monde"[1866] and Whistler's "Symphony in white. No.1: The White Girl." [1871]

Non-Verbalized Foreplay

Irrelevance of subject of their conversation.
No idea of the type of coffee ordered.
Status of audio-visual for presentation... gleefully relegated.

Not the slightest interest
in airline luggage size of overheads, for next trip.

Short term and long planning nonchalantly intermingled:
This second... next second...
... or the rest of his life.

Past intimacies or next week end party.
Time...
had become a pre-Big-Bang mass of possibilities.

Across the plastic and metal cafeteria table,
her presence...
had opened an emotional black hole.

No outside sounds, breaking through the lunchroom cocoon:
The eerie silence filled with only one vibration:
her voice.

As though protected by divine intervention:
Fearlessly walking in traffic to their respective jobs.

Chastely embracing
—somehow feeling their secret already out—

Their lives... like their bodies,
Seen as already intertwined.

In this...
the eternally unspoken... unwritten contract:
that only lovers can decipher.

White collar professionals at the Genesis of their relationship.

First Glance

In between the immediate and the perceived
lives the eternally desired.

Between the sweaty morning visions of vanishing exhaustion
and the pursing of lips,
begins... already... the swelling waves of regrets
and the longing for the precious value
of what has just taken place.

Simple... natural things can engender such access
to very peculiar wormholes of the human heart and mind...
a rumor,
an entrance,
a glance away from a copying machine.

And a multidimensional
explosion into unlimited possibilities!

A greeting... from a voice seemingly from the best musical lines
of Romantics around the shores of lake Como.

A voice... offering the feel of the silky warmth
from the scented Maghrebian world of engorged prickly pears
found in the solar universe of Camus.

Or a ride on the asymptotes of unrequited loves of Stendhal.

Heartbreaking moments full, of the intelligent sensuality
of characters sensitive to the flawless quality of rare emotions.
And its gradations between pregnant expectation,
reserve, and abandonment...
Complete and unconditional abandonment...

———————————————————————

... all and any of the above
came to his mind, with each step, on his way to shake her hand.

Empty Shell

Remark made by a 1960's university classmate, now a retuning Viet Nam veteran: "I left full of the best of Western philosophers and came back empty."

He had read about these out of body moments:
"crazy people" he thought.

Two places at once…
looking at your body from another person's view.

The stuff of nineteenth century poets he had studied:
The flowers of primordial dung and evil.
"Emanations from various dopes found in Parisians parlors,"
he would snicker.

And yet,
here he was… in a car that would no longer be his, the very next day.
A willing, cute, pliable co-ed:
The type of situation youth prays for.

She represented, within inches, all that he would no longer have:
All his cravings turning into a sadistic mirage.

A sort of hedonistic, sacrilegious, nihilistic Moses:
Within striking distance of his goal.

"And not a god in sight" … to take away his Promise Land, this time!
No keeper of the *book* of ethics, around. This back seat is not Sinai!
No stern maternal look, with its years of righteous guidance.
And…
All the time, he was facing the indoctrination of boot-camp.
That hallow ritual that prepares the flesh to kill flesh
and historians to wrap blood in flags of glory.

Except… except…
for the foreseen pain…to be inflicted on this girl.
Still… *She* in love with what he represented up to the minute
before he had opened his mail.

A draft letter...
that would lead to stolen tomorrows and negated yesterdays.

A cosmos gone mad: all these people and things,
crashing into each other to produce a vicious universe,
in the back of a Volkswagen.

He would replay it, many times:

... She had lustfully reclined in the back seat.

Thoughts...
without tomorrows by both.
Thoughts...
without lessons from of old celibate priests.
Thoughts...
of a mother's unconditional forgiveness and love.
Thoughts...
that evil can and does invade the righteous heart.
Leaving you to rationalize the rest of your life.

He gently brought her back up,
Perplexed by their mutual, non-verbalized... non-sexual embrace:
Chasing away visons of his contemplated brutality upon her.

Draftee on last date before going to boot camp.

Artistic Rage

Homage to Camille Claudel.

Sensuality of engorged lips kissing.
Undercurrent of perceptible nervous energy.
Indentation of fingertips into the pliable lower back of an embrace.

Immortalized moments of happiness
rendered by the alchemy of the *living* mineral solidity of marble.

All this ferment of human passion,
still transfixing the passing museum visitor.

A quasi miraculous talent by the artist
to have transmitted life into the *inert*:
In the manner of a divined digit.

And yet, cosmological enemies
—like some vulgar matter to its ethereal antimatter—
lived in this frail and susceptible soul.

Her fingers were transmitting poetic visions
With every febrile movement of the chisel.

While a self-loathing seeped
from the black corners of a very human self-doubt.

Unspeakable rage, in such a lyrical soul,
having set unreachable beauty and intimate happiness as her firmament.

And so…like some enraged Assyrian potentate on his burning funeral
pyre, she set to kill her stone-children.

Victim of the ultimate anti-Christ of any artist:
the feeling of lyrical abandonment.

A beautiful soul, no longer seeing its reflection
in the glance in her morning mirror.

The fate of too many tender,
multicolored, multifaceted individuals…
… in a flat and colorless world.

Gaël Le Cornec: about Camille Claudel, a student artist who reached—and arguably outdid—her patron, August Rodin, and his belief that: "… she [Camille Claudel] languished here [in an insane asylum] for decades for being a woman who was 'ahead of her time'."

Tragedy, Despair and Hope.

"The terrible thing about death is that it transforms life into destiny." (André Malraux)

The enormous granite basement blocks
Had quietly been standing guard around the metal anchors of the machines.
Men… had been there… and had disappeared.

A Gothic dignity still permeated the dampness:
A place of respectful reflection at the transept of agony and hope.

Everything conspired to bring you back to the elemental truths:
Men live. Men die. Others survive.

The killing water, that had invaded the space:
just a metaphor, in spite of the ignorance of its own power.
Of its role in the *human condition*.

A place of contradiction:
Removing the dead from its present… adding them to a living future.
A watery grave, to turn the wheel of dreams and accomplishments.

Distance… between these two men, measured by continents
And yet, calculated by heartbeats,
In a secular prayer born of human solidarity.

Inspired by a visit, at the site of a deadly flood in a former New England mill: where one man's tragic death was the source of a new immigrant's future and his progeny.

Of Witchcraft and Womanhood

It must have been in her eyes:
A hint of arrogance. The hesitation to follow a man's whim.

The insulting habit of contradicting with a slow response.
The unmitigated gall of doing something more efficiently than men could.

Where did this ability come from?
Was she communicating with Lucifer when, during the night,
she would leave… the nuptial bed crying?

What if her ilk in the village banded together?

What of the evidence of their unhuman ability?
How can a person regularly bleed so much and not die?

She will pay for such arrogance!

The way difficult slaves would eventually die:
For looking directly into their masters' eyes.

Independence: the insidious, unnatural trait in women often accused of being witches.

Splendid Silence

Two older women,
ingots along the quieter, lower sandy banks of a mountain torrent.

Precious… regurgitated—would-be forgotten—
innards of history:

The ones…too coarse, too troublesome to pass downstream.
Overlooked.

———————————————

Wrinkled re-incarnations of dark historical memories.
Witnesses and victims to repulsive ugliness.

Fully covered with the secular stigmata
of disillusioned sororities of their respective faiths.

Quasi-mutes… witnesses to too much…
with too much to say.

———————————————

Now… sitting across one from the other,
in splendid silence.

Imparting an air of miraculous kosher status over the kitchen,
by their very presence.

The flow of precious memories
seemingly transmitted telepathically.

———————————————

The maid had inquisitively pointed
to a blueish porcelain figurine:
Surviving piece of the family's Berlin apartment:
provoking a stream of tears in the otherwise cold exterior of her employer.

Followed in turn,
by the fragility of a faded black and white picture from the maid's wallet:
A smiling little girl with her parents, weeks before the air-raids.

Two women… strangers to their new worlds.
With respective feral instincts of survival:
Detecting a biblical wisdom,
born of the purity of human kindness in the other's glance:
Somehow codified by their respective suffering.

All in the quiet ritual of a thick, black coffee:
at the majesty of a minuscule card table.

Newly arrived in America, a devout Roman Catholic immigrant, brutalized by the Nasi occupation of France, becomes a maid and befriends the lady of the house (of a German refugee) in a strictly observing Jewish home (circa early 1950's). The former speaks little English, while the latter's is heavily Yiddish-accented.

Dying: First Person Singular

The setting: Russian winter, 1953. A dacha in the suburb of Moscow. Stalin is dying.

Did he feel
the eyes of the ghosts of his victims on him?
A welcoming committee
for his kind who had preceded him?

The mere mortals among us
Used to die in the hazy gaze of his family
Around the most comfortable bed in the house.

Kings and despots, on the other hand,
often die for an historical audience:
It is an unappealable statement
of death's even-handed... unsentimental power.

Death's complete supremacy
over this last human act.

Taking away all... and every accoutrement of
privilege, whims, and self-aggrandizement.

Absolute impartiality reigns in the nature of this last human rite.

No letter of nobility. No credentials. No wax seals.
No exception... on this side of a universe with no Big-Bang residues of
recourse to accommodating divinities.

Ah! But for the torturer's last instants
to be filled by phantasmagoric visions!

Inspired by "Le roi se meurt" by Eugène Ionesco.

Prodigal **Moment**

Irresistibly drawn to *her,*
Despite university Enlightenment having invaded his soul.
Resisting the urge, with every instinct of rationalism.

He had made his way to the enormous mass of stones.
Hesitating. Last steps.

The spiritual and physical emptiness of the last feet,
in spite of the touristic multitude.

He finds the strength
to break a quasi-*respectful cordon of privacy* around *her.*

Amidst a moral brew of academic idealism,
sprinkled with affected Left Bank fatalism:

Finding himself quasi naively…
with a hint of teenage awkward stupidity,
for anything distant, untouchable
… and beautiful.

He now tries to focus on *her* gray roughness.

One last look sideways,
to forgo possible snickers.

Literally exhausted…
extending his left palm.

Caressing the ageless solidity:
Looking straight up at the tower.

An apotheosis takes over:
All and nothing could exist in the same place and time;
Shameless religiosity.

And the transcendence of eternal beauty.

He thought:
"I wonder, if upon touching the stone,
the fearful shrieks of those monkeys of *Space Odyssey*,
had found the same thing?

Returning French expatriate, back in Paris after decades of absence: now a thorough
non-believer, he is drawn to the left tower of Notre Dame de Paris.
This poem was written years before the 2019 fire.

And... Societies Invented Sex

Our haunting, past identities had been there all along:
Our dual nature...
Alternatively, vaporous... idealistic;
Or visceral... animalistic.

Kant and the Marquis de Sade,
explorers of these antithetical and complementary worlds:

Literature weaving dark tales of fiction
of seductive Transylvanian counts and conflicted Frankenstein creations.

Illuminated religious zealots like the lecherous Monsignor Frollo:
Unreconciled with his body's sexual impulses
and the meaning of his archdeacon vestments.

We continue to ignore, in our morning mirror such tangible evidence
as the hairy vestiges of our cave people-selves.

Catching, in side glimpses, puffs of body hair
around the cottony whiteness of the bath towel:

Those patches of primate protection from our savannah days.

We perfume and spray areas:
Sources of bodily pheromone scent from vestigial glands.
And then serenely put on our Italian cotton office suits.

Our sexual animal-self resurfaces,
When eyeing the opposite sex in the high-tech jungle
of internet dating and cocktail hours.

Nature's side of our nature.
Un-apologetical.
Sex... by name...
... a built-in necessity for survival of the specie,
with no more ethical weight than our daily hunger.

Squids and termites not evolved enough to have codified
their manners of reproduction.
But... primates... have.

Thus... rut entered human consciousness
as some of the most memorable, lustful moments of literature and law.

With such men and women,
in impeccable designer suits, intoxicating perfumes
and lipstick worthy of any forest plumage.

Fine cotton and finer hoses.
Advance degrees and wedding bans.
Regal oaths and professional taboos... floating high above it all.

Thousand pages of deterrents and traditions.
Tales and threats of scarlet letters and absolute loss of pride and respect.

And societies... still unable to insulate the cloth-covered flesh
from the danger represented by the gargoyle-spouts of Notre Dame de Paris.

Inspired by another sex scandal involving an, heretofore, irreproachable "pillar" of the community.

Cellulose Fragility

To the memory of the iconic Alexandria library.

Quaint arrogance of man… and his kind:
Pathetically weak in his individual fate.
Fate…
… made of mortal flesh, saddled to limitless visions of himself.
Himself…
… driven to contemplate, conceive and construct.
Construct…
… using the density of seemingly eternal stones…
Stones…
… of perfectly quarried-stones upon stones.
Stones…
… to man's collective glory, by imprinting an ephemeral presence.
Presence…
… pushing through the sands, deltas and palm-groves,
All…
… silent witnesses to embryonic civilizations:
made of aligned columns and engraved peristyles.
Peristyles…
… high above already existing sacred grounds,
geometrically defined in glorious solar squares.
Solar squares…
… henceforth, gathered around this consecrated distillation of knowledge.
Knowledge…
made of rolls of papyruses, aligned in silence;

As they dare, in cellulose fragility,
challenge the dumb immensity of time.

Fuite dans le vide

Echappée en Renault 16 sur les départementales circa 1968.

Échos de moments de pure insouciance,
comme seule la jeunesse nous le permet.

Nourris par une réserve inépuisable de bonheur à perte de vue :
« Et tout ce temps pour le boire. »

« Je t'aime... moi non plus. »
Formule des enfants de ce siècle.
Formule... dite et répétée sans trop vraiment y croire.

Un monde à tout refaire et à oublier.
Des serments à renier et des cœurs à trahir.

Trajet et trajectoire sans boussole :
Guidés par les pages séculaires d'un Michelin.

———————————————

Déjeuners pleins de paganisme médiéval.
Guidés par la valeur immortelle de ce petit mur de pierre.

C'était là...
dans la congruence des choses... bonnes et belles,
que ce talisman s'est laissé offrir aux happy few .

Une bouteille de Cahors qui... avec une certaine pudeur,
à commencer à se déshabiller de son étiquette :

Exhibant, à travers son effacement, l'éphémère du moment.

*Réflexions sur une photographie montrant deux hommes assis contre un mur de pierres
avec leur bouteille de Cahors 1947.*

Flight Into the Void

Escape in a Renault 16 on the local roads. (France) circa 1968

Echoes of moments of pure recklessness,
as only youth would allow.

Nourished by an unending source of happiness:
"And all that time to drink it!"

"I love you... neither do I"
On the movie marquis about the children of this century.
Mottos... pronounced and repeated with not much conviction.

A world to be completely rebuilt and soon forgotten.
Oaths to be reneged and hearts to be cheated.

Treks and trajectories without compass;
Guided by the secular pages of the Michelin guide..

———————————————

Lunches full of medieval paganism,
Guided by the immortal worth of this little stone wall.

It was there...
in the congruity of things ... good and beautiful,
that this talisman allowed itself to be gifted to the happy few:

A bottle of Cahors which... with a certain reserve,
started to undress itself of its label:
exhibiting, through its very timidity, the ephemeral nature of the moment.

Reflections on a photograph of two men sitting against a stone wall showing their 1947 bottle of Cahors.

Homage to a 1964' Volkswagen

Between the immediate and the perceived…
…lives the desired:

The former was made of minutes, instinct and embraces,
Found in the nuptial darkness of a home-coming prom.

A ritual…
protected by a teenage arrogance, that somehow
—by steamy efforts—
would eternally keep out a New England February night.

All… as a part of a timeless carnal Genesis.

In his later years… the repulsive paper dullness of an office expense report,
would make memories
from the fertile organic smells of those kisses.

That very human…
No!… solely human trait of longing.

Time and space,
that we now try to fill with a wiser arrogance.

This void… mankind's awareness… and the artist.

Remembering oblivious teenage happiness.

I Will Miss...

I will miss the taste of the earthy aroma of grapes...
from the very innocence of fermentation.

Bordeaux... and the quieting heat of the Fall sun
on the sleepy oyster-fields of the Atlantic.

The purple sparkle contained in glassy transparence:
Itself contained by a left hand... as though in an attempt to extend
happiness.

I will miss anticipation itself:
A particularly human trait that measures the value of time.

That hedonistic satisfaction,
In the friction between the solidity of reality and its eternal lost,
found at the limit of exhaustion.

I will miss the simplicity and frustration of seconds:
And yet, their ease into continuity.

The spectacular... found in the mundane.

The human nobility of receiving acknowledgment from a simple smile:
And its acknowledgement among a thousand others
in the anonymity of an international departure.

I will miss the natural, animal informality, hidden in the next minutes
filled by touching hips: in the deadly coldness of office hours.

And the... elementary religiosity of a simple family meal,
without demanding its human price in eternal dogma.

An un-abridged stream of consciousness wish-list.

Like Job...

A fable

The living body...finished with its living:
Getting ready to appear in front of the cold disinterest of a blind universe.
No need for painterly mannerisms... elemental honesty will do.

The weakest and ugliest molecules of withered flesh,
Still...
Somehow... infused ... with memories of perfumed essences
from the hills of Provence...
Still intertwined with the nervous feel of intimate silky flesh
of Parisian carnal days.

Facing now, the immemorial human act of going home from the temporary.
The corpse readying for its dissipation, back into the dust of stellar womb.

Bodily marks from the repulsive abuse of years shown
on the blotted abdomen.
Distended veins, mindlessly, pumping out a tired, serpentine boredom.

And yet, the immeasurable heartbreaking dignity!
Resigned abandonment: captured in a quasi-receptive male femininity.
Alabaster rendering of the skin in a language of asexual muscular
emaciation:
Standing for nothing...
But the immortal truths... disappearing on the melting wax of earthy slates.

All this flow of stoic wisdom,
Seemingly entering his quasi disincarnated body,
In flashes of light, through translucent eyes.

Recurring visions, made of secretive memories:
Intimate, youthful, nubile frissons of anticipation of the next minutes,
In miniscule bedrooms overlooking Montmartre.

Those golden, sensual moments...
punctuated by explicit life-giving groans:

Stingy gifts of nature's glory.
Golden, sensual moments… of human happiness,
by now…
Parading invisibly above his solitary loins.

Job, surrounded by his earthly goods:
Composed of fewer people and even fewer things:
A bee…
Still flying in the late autumn coolness.
At his calloused feet… oblivious black ants,
Wandering nervously in the sterile desert dust:
Deluded animals becoming the center of his world.

A *Sartrean nausea* invades his solidarity with these beasts.
Equivalences in cosmological equations that somehow condense
Droplets of human thoughts on translucent wings and spindly legs.

Nudity…
Politely and gently… Obediently and naturally…
Attaching itself to dust, insects and nothingness.

Reconstructing Léon Bonnat, "The Prophet Job," as a hedonist in a nihilistic universe.

Profile in Clair-Obscur

Homage to Jacques Louis David

Clair-obscur into the gentle sweetness of youth,
where innocence does not know the landscape
on the outside of the gates of Eden.

A place of emotional tranquility,
where even Lucifer is transfixed into his original self:
as God's favorite, not yet aware of his cosmic attraction.

Moments… places… and person… magically incarnated
from the best moments of the story of earthly life:

Limitless riches,
found in the natural plasticity in the crimson of flesh.

All in a visual congruence,
that captures the frustrating sight of perfection:
in a foretelling découpage of darkness.

Based on picture profile, in strong chiaroscuro contrast, of a young girl.

Reincarnations

"It is with such eyes ... that a pair of angels exiled among men ... gaze at one another in mutual recognition." (Stendhal [Henri Beyle]), in Armance.

It was, somehow, irrationally… the same eyes.
The same glance.
As though, pursued by the Devil himself… *Herself.*

The pursuit of love, having the impossible power over photons and mortals,
To change his entrance into a room:

Giving a miserable fourth floor dormitory room
the expanse of clouds trying to fill the sky on a hot humid afternoon…
invading every corner of everything.

Making the otherwise frightening awareness of carnal hunger
So often found in teenage glances
The words of a language spoken to his younger self.

He is now facing a pregnant Sphinx-like silence from an Odalys-pose
on a lumpy Parisian mattress:
Replacing the real one from a museum wall.

These different girls… on different continents:
Icons of his *sentimental education.*

Distinct ages and cultures:
Each and all, apparently different in flesh… and yet, carnally, so similar.

A timeless, flint-like emanation. The immortal steely self-assurance of
Grecian statues.
An uncompromising refusal of any hint into the suspected richness and
savor of their inner life.

From the awkward presences of his barely post puberty…
… to the magic of a self-scripted courtisane from les liaisons *dangereuses,*
He later realized, that… these so often-maligned gods of his universe,
Had privileged his senses to be receptive to those moments:

When the dumb wisdom of evolution,
in glorious instants of eternity…

—and violating all laws of cosmology—

… meets the lyricism of sentient happiness:
Through the mere —but very human—need of artistically ignoring time.

He never forgot her appearance in his life, as a young man. Leaving him searching for that moment… in all the others thereafter.

The Myth of the Amoebae

Philosophy on a bed in Paris (circa 1960's)

He:
I've been thinking…

She:
Shit!

He:
No! No…listen: this is exactly the time and the place.

She:
You have got to be kidding!
After what has just happened on these sheets?! Is this what you were thinking of all the time?
I'm going to throw this cheap ashtray at you.

He:
Take it easy… it could be a museum piece… don't forget this is Paris…
I have heard that hotel owners get their room furnishing from the marchés aux puces: like les Puces de Saint-Ouen. And they sometimes come up with estate material… unnoticed…
Why just last year…

She:
Oh! shut up.

He:
Anyway … first of all I was fully concentrating on things… second … this place… and what we just finished doing, is EXACTLY appropriate for what I was thinking… or rather what we were doing MADE me think… it really reminded me of what I have been toying with.

She:
[sitting up against the head board of the bed—bringing her knees to her breasts—locking her fingers on the top of her shinbones—parts of her are still shimmering despite the relative obscurity between her thighs].
I'm all ears.

He:
Among other things.

She:
Espèce de con!

He:
Well here it is…
It is going to be the topic of a little article that I am going to send out.
It's called the "Myth of the amoebae."

She:
It wouldn't be about some of the administrators of the university by any chance?

He:
No… this is about higher life.
Anyway… I envision a place in the bowels of some rock formation of the earth; or in the depth of the ocean: basically, a spot on the globe where scientists were surprised…more like stupefied… to have found "living' cellular activity.
Life… living! The continuation of life.

She:
You mean what we would have done if…

He:
Yeah… Yeah…
But listen… Not just stupid mineral existence, solidified cosmic dust!
There were reports, for instance, of incredibly toxic vents at the bottom of the ocean that were spewing hot content from the earth crust: sort of hot springs of chemicals, water and evidence of organic material: pre-DNA stuff.

If Kant and other philosophers were interested in the question of "consciousness": what its sources could be and what it means to our idea of our awareness of life [our awareness of awareness in a nut shell].

My article would agree to simply accept the premise that this consciousness is a given; but then… look at it from the outside.

So, now… let us say that we had evidence of entities, a 'living world" of some sort… and now let us say that we are entities within it… entities aware of their own presence in this world.

How would these entities see other presences within this world and how could they go or (project) outside of themselves, in order to do it?
For to think about these questions, the entities would have to use… let us say, their brains. These brains are made of the material at hand.

The stuff that gave them life; and that has evolved into living things… that have consciousness… and IS MADE of the very material that these entities want to study.

Now. Here's the thought experiment… suppose… that these Amoebas are us. How is this possible. How can you project (as an Amoebae in the depth of the ocean) … how can you project beyond where… and what you are? It would be the intellectual equivalent of operating on yourself?

How can these Amoebas envision a world outside of theirs; if all they know, is the hot deep-water vents where they have evolved?

What is … "what is not them" in another world?
And it is not a question of some science fiction world. That's easy!

It is the stuff of talented Hollywood script-writers who can envision other worlds.

These worlds are just other worlds in which other things exist which are just as clueless as to where their intelligence comes from.

More fundamentally, for instance: who controls the whole machinery of the universe?
Or the given of "accepted constants."
Such as, why a speed of light?
Why a speed of light through billion of light years, practically immune to anything?
Why should there be a speed of light?
Why should there be anything in the first place?
See? that is why I allow myself the pleasure that has taken place on this bed to distract me form all of this.

A sort of sensory, hedonistic overload of the flesh to distract my mind away from overload.

The Garden of Eden… Revisited

From the triangle of flesh
and its bold vertical arrow in the cloth,
Pointing to a parting pout and Esmeralda glance.

Sinuous twist of the stance,
complementing the tempting dangerous curvature of the fingers.

Primordial vision,
frightening only to those who divide happiness from living.

Pre-ethical moment,
when good and evil added to no more than the act of breathing.

Luxurious Garden… full of natural peace,
between nudity and the sweetly sour taste of an engorged fruit.

Silently stunned before this emanating hedonism:
Of what is a very human and purely human vision.

Earthy happiness…
that continues to feed the vaporous envy of the gods.

Inspired by bold colored ink drawing of suggestive figure, in black silky dress, beckoning the viewer.

The Birth of Time

We are inside the clock mechanism
Somehow trying to define
what all these wheels and springs mean to our lives.

Somehow having
the arrogance of knowledge… *of true knowledge.*
Not semblance: such the earth flatness.

The solidity of the bronze and rock of the naked form
Having no means to stray beyond itself.

A sigh of capitulation leaves the viewer:
"Time started when matter began to change in time."

It took the artist and his art to compress
Beauty…
into a primordial… marble… singularity.

Reflection on a visit of Le penseur (the Thinker) at the musée Rodin in Paris.

The Lady Across the Inlet

Death of a young black man, on the gritty New Jersey side, within sight of the Statue of Liberty. [Loosely inspired by the movie "Seven Seconds"]

All of these scenes of despair…
all of them, playing on the screen of our guilty souls.

The land of opportunity…
for brand-new immigrants, with brand new hearts:
Dancing in vapors of hope and renewal.

Chiaroscuro between the light-green fragility of reeds
And the dividing slashes of blood stains…
straight from the palette of Caravaggio.

Unbridled shredding of human flesh by lead bullets.
Baby carriages… swept aside by surrealistic moments of addictive violence.

Subhuman world of alternative evolution of existence
where Lucifer would have gloriously won the battle.

_____

This teenager had lost the fight
long before the blade had entered his flank:

Having been taken off the breast of hope,
long before his own mother's death.

So that his last glance,
through the morning mist and joyful *peepers,*
would be toward the golden reflection on the torch…

… Unaware of the heartbreaking distance to *Her*.

To the theme of "Superfly" by Curtis Mayfield

Poets, Cosmologists and Dreamers

Homage to Steven Hawking.

Not unlike a skinny teenager, after his first kiss:
His chest ready to explode from the after tremors.

Now feeling like on a stallion:
During his return home from the beach on his bicycle.

A blur of contradictory emotions:
She had hinted at something… just before the event…
A collapsing of Time into a singularity,
on this mundane beach, now seemingly overlooking endless opportunities.

A coy tightening of the corners of her lips
A summery conversation of iconic value
whose details he would try to replay.

Did they accidentally brush?
Did their thighs touch under the beach table?

What could he have said to could have produced this?
What parts of her body in her diminutive bikini counted more?

What future images did he see in her brownish hazel eyes
which he thought blue?

He would return often to this bench,
In the warmth of Proustian instants,
In emotional wanderings, facing away from his classes
While constructing frigid consumption curves per household.

Drifting into his youth while driving past this beach,
Among billions in the cosmos
Source of billions of memories
On some cold New England February night;

Or… Angered at himself for seeing her ghostly presence in his wife's smile.

Trying to ethically give their parts of life to the living
To his present…
so as to not diminish either and live in illusions of alternate futures.

What molecules of reality now in his arms
could he continue to count on?

And so did the physicist having tried to bend time
go to his death, still looking back…
to moments of thirst for that kiss…
in a very personal, intimate, and very human victory.

Could there be a similarity between the dreamy-eyed poet and the computer code-driven physicist: both use their respective tools—vaporous lyricism for the first and tangled formulae for the latter—to get to their truth, the hardcore of their reality, the genesis of their subjects: Time?

Unless in a universe where it is not so, Time starts and is part of a forward movement of physics [i.e. change of matter in time]. While for some deluded poets, Time can start with the moment of "the first kiss." Both the writers and scientists have been trying to swim back to those beginnings. [Hawking died on March 2018]

The Unapproachable

It was so natural…
She was sitting on the sand next to him:
Yves Montand was playing on the new "transistor" radio.

His father's glistening muscular back
gliding off the beach of the Pointe Rouge.

His mother starting a "brandade" with her best aromatic oil.

… He is proudly taking a video
with the background noise of the wavelets and cicada.
His children in silhouette against the beach stones.
And the heat…
the generous heat of the Provençal sun!

A religious beatitude permeated the scene:
His nihilistic soul, at ease,
under the gaze of "la Bonne Mère."

Mother and her Child
looking down from her hill.

… He woke up:
His summers in Marseille, with Uncle Raoul,
long ago evaporated.

The acrimonious pettiness of "big persons" inheritance problems,
Sterilized by the heat and filtered with age.

He was still in the multi-dimensional world
Between sleep and the reality…
driving in the snow of New England.

Reflection in a Mirror

Hotel room, by Place de Clichy, Paris (May, 1968)

She whispered:
"Don't you think you should take a taxi? It's raining."

He could see her reflection in the mirror.
He chose instead to continue looking into it.

She was just behind him,
sitting upright with her knees to her chest:
draped in the bed sheet.

Her voice seemed to come from the walls of the room.
Her image… on the glass… appeared somehow more real
than her flesh a few feet away.

"Don't worry; it's always romantic to walk in Paris."

The question and the answer had been
ridiculously unconnected to the emotions of the moment.

Who cared about the mode of travel
that would be the beginning of separation?

Why add that painful lyrical reference
to the belated impact of this city?

They were at the exit gates
of accidental happiness.

They knew it…
and neither one had enough faith in an idealized future
that would change anything about the next few minutes.

Prelude to unstoppable moments of heartbreak.

Meursault in Love

IT …had supported him through the emotional voids.
The plaintive groans of cancerous death,
through paper-thin walls.

Through the ethical choices
of conceding to kill for the color of one's uniform.

―――――――――――――――

Having absorbed the clear-eyed philosophy of a divinity-free universe:
he had discovered being left to depend on his own compass.

The gentle, solar voice
of the author, the narrator… the man,
had assumed the role of oracle of human wisdom:
replacing the one of the catechisms of his youth.

―――――――――――――――

He had found the same visceral and symbolic attraction of the flesh,
while reading l'Été à Tipasa:

Echoing the warmth
of the Maghrebian sun on naked bodies.

Like a previous "prophet" of books,
Meursault had suffered and paid dearly for his
way of *dealing* with emptiness.

―――――――――――――――

All had been safely and conveniently folded
for his academic, personal and messianic travels.

Until this confessional glance
into the nature of the next minutes
in the life of the quasi-god of his curriculum.

A figure… that gave human courage
while facing super-unhuman philosophical odds.
A man of personal and intellectual integrity,
having written of his touching anxiety for the next minute "without her."

Pathetically tender words.
Absolute righteousness in a hopeless cause.
The great writer himself.
Alone in his room.
And his heart aching.

This author, who dared to unblinkingly look
into the intellectual abyss of eternity.

Now... single-mindedly interested
in the few hours before "seeing her again."

The great Albert Camus!
With the passion of a teen-ager
—unburdened with infinity—

Wide awake in his bed.
Waiting... simply for sunrise.
Her embrace. Perfume and glance.

With what would pass-off
as sordid religiosity.
As intellectual dishonesty,
in anyone less un-impeachable.

So that
—even in a god-less cosmos—
we are, sometimes, made to understand
how early Christians stood, with an understated smile,
in front of enraged African lions.

*Nota bene. Albert Camus, who could qualify for god-like standing in university students'
heart, reveals himself unashamedly at the level of a Freshman, having dropped-off his
date at her dormitory.*

Of Secular Prophets

To the memory of Albert Camus (On a cliff in North Africa).

Like clouds of incense, floating in a cavernous stony holy of holies,
he spoke among whiffs of acrid fumes of French Gauloises.

He still lives… in the poetry of the gentle Mediterranean Sea
and the prose of history…

… In the aroma of distilled oils from late summer flowers,
catching a cooling whistling sea breeze over the Corinthian columns:
Solidly guarding the elysian fields of his youth, he loved.

He still lives… within sight of the indelible memories of moist skins
touching each other in their glorious nudity…

… The white saltiness of the sea replacing the grittiness of grains of
sands, reminding them of earthy reality.

He is the secular prophet within whom burned the passion
of all lovers of truth and righteousness.

Aware of the danger of absolutes.
Aware of the exquisite fragility of life:
These precepts acting as religious beliefs in a non-religious man.

He spoke in words with the quasi solidity
and adaptable descriptive powers of poetic prose:

Always conscious of the antithetical dilemma
inherent of the immortality of truth…
in a deaf and dumb universe.

A consummate artist who testified for the beautiful:
In words that real lovers have never tired of expressing.

Not unlike the repetitive rhythmic chants of primitive mankind.
Chants that could somehow dare to modify the physical universe.

Real prophets speak often in contradictions
and much before their time:
Guided by their own scale of time.

Un-afraid of the momentary peculiarities of political dogmas.
Or established religious taboos.
Not shy of disturbing and forming their own space continuum.

Often preaching in deserts:
with scorpions as their first intrigued audience.

They knew that time was on their side.
And that the grains of flying sand would expose the real intent
hidden in the underlayers of chiseled words:
On the original surface of the tombstone.

We have to picture Camus as unconcerned
by his status as the accidental prodigal son in his own birthplace.

Poets and prophets of the truth are passionate lovers of thoughtful integrity:
Reaching on asymptotes toward untouchable infinity.

And like all secular lovers, unhindered by canonic laws of man…
reserving "the right to love without limits or conventions."

Simone Veil

A fable

Le beau est ce qu'on ne peut pas vouloir changer.
Beauty is what one does not want changed.
(Simone Veil, "Une vie")

In a corner of the eternal cosmos:
A place so removed from conscience and the conscious,
that things are at their elementary neutral.

A place of absolute ethics and justice,
that must have preceded the Big-Bang.

A place where the religious and canonic
are no match for the noble blanching effect of indescribable silence.

A place... at the limit of a what would have been
if a perfect expansion... into a *perfect space*...
had been made *from perfect pieces.*

Where, therefore...
evenhanded nothingness would have existed all along.

A place where Simone and her kind must now be living:
a place of no memory of the atrocities and unkindness they have suffered.

In the name of societies' concept of perfection.

The ultimate indecent irony towards Simone Viel, Shoah survivor, who had witnessed
her mother dying in her arms at the liberation of their concentration camp and the
incomprehensible horror of industrial size murder: being accused as a murderer, during
her defense, in parliament, of women's right to reproductive choice.

Queen Liliuokalani

Addendum to Alexis de Tocqueville's "On Democracy in America."

Like some sort of fresh produce,
Democracy should exhibit a "sale-by date."

A "Use it" … or "Lose it date":
On this, a sweetly-gentle, fairy-tale island:

Where sugar refiners and pineapple growers,
will play the part of the electoral college.

Depending on his entrance
into the various pages of U.S. history,
a visitor could have witnessed abject slavery
or the cleansing winds of constitutional democracy.

A civil war in the past of the main land.

While on the land of flowers of Paradise,
lush green mountains
and images of the original Eden:
kept such…
in benign innocence by an endless ocean.

Or so it would have been,
if not for societies' taste
for the addictive sweetness.

And thus…for a quaint monarchy,
in the slightly over-weight figure of a queen,
thoughts of the white purity of democracy
was not appreciated.

A feminine figure of motherland authority:
for a kingdom of gentle tropical winds.

Properly and legally invaded.
Dethroned by political scions
of the greatest representative democracy:
in clouds of sugar crystals...
making the bitter irony go down.

On January 17th 1893, Hawaii's monarchy was overthrown when a group of businessmen and sugar planters forced Queen Liliuokalani to abdicate. The coup led to the dissolving of the Kingdom of Hawaii, its annexation as a U.S. territory and eventual admission as the 50th state in the union.

Horrors and Ethereal Notes

In homage to Amnon Weinstein: les violons de la Shoah

In a magical conspiracy…
the vibrating fingers on the neck of the instruments,
seemed to pry molecules of tears from the wood.

A symbiosis of the memory, imprisoned in the varnished cellulose,
forced passive witness to horrors…
now released as ethereal notes.

The whole, a recombined construct,
of phantasmagoric cold and evil shadows in the gothic darkness,
bouncing off the granite orchestra floor.

———————————————

Like many moralistic tales told to children,
the fear and tears produced by the searing vibrato of the narration,
are mankind's way that give solidity
to the hours of cold darkness and pure evil.

The hours of cold darkness and pure evil.

Inspired by a musical event, in Dresden, on "surviving" instruments from victims of the Shoah. The instruments, played in the concentration camps, were given "new life" by Amnon Weinstein, an Israeli luthier.

Tralfamadorian Man

A fable

"Te revoir encore une fois…
serait savoir que je te perdrai une fois de plus."

"Seeing you once more…
would be knowing that I will lose you one more time."

A Tralfamadorian man reliving the joys… and pain of his past.

Sidi Moussa, Salé, Morocco (circa 1954)

He knew… he knew,
for having lived and relived them,
that *things* had come accidently together.

Producing yet again,
a logical sequence of events of his past.
—they always had—

When… like a Doctor Faust… writing, alone… late at night,
yielding to temptation.
Yielding…
to the uncontrollable passion of holding her once more.

His words would, henceforth, transpose him randomly
on the arc of his existence:
allowing him a quasi-divine *second taste* at life.

Not unlike, bringing forth the past,
found in the vanillin perfume of *Proustian* madeleines,
in whiffs from the kitchen.

He would, henceforth,
reappear at this street corner,
after "words had been exchanged in the school hallway"
a block from his old neighborhood:

or...
he would drive again around the forgotten sharp right
in the New England darkness:
Intoxicated with plans for the week end.
or...
in the ultimate dispensation from linear time:
have a second chance... at the *preceding instant* just before
the untouched purity of their first kiss:

That supreme chance of an eternal glance
Upon the closing of her eyelashes.

He felt emboldened...
No more fear from the destructive nature of time:
The bottomless abyss, home of dead and dying human happiness.

"Art and the artist can vanquish time":
A hellish presence in crimson silks,
whispered from across his writing desk.

He had lived, up to that moment... inside the bounds
of ordinary events and ordinary people:
Everything evolving, seamlessly, in only one direction: Forward:

Inanimate things... waves of people, intersected only once:
Sparing, for the rest of us, mere mortals,
the pain of the repetition of agonies or joys.

But condemning, the ardent *Happy Few*,
to simply accept their unanswered cravings for more visits
to their personal happiness.

Alone in the alchemic world of fiction:
reflecting, with a sniff of *fine de Champagne Cognac,*
on this forward and un-stoppable nature of the universe:
He took that lyrical leap:

It was a sort of escape hatch, where human creative needs
allow the mind to invent idealized worlds.

Worlds that could find the writer's feet in a frozen dacha of Russian cold,
while the creative genius of *a* lovelorn Doctor Zhivago
could conceive *a* lubricious Lara in bed, under furs.

So that... now... at his desk,
in his *created realities*, he is omnipotent.

Both things and people, voluntarily... consciously
But... apparently, erratically and stupidly,
would henceforth allow him:

To step out, once more... unto that street.

To hold again, the steering wheel.

To feel, in his old age, the iodized wind invades. once more,
the fateful grotto, on this Maghrebian beach.

While... leaning against the back wall...
her fixating glance... her deep dark fixating glance...
would, once more, block any attempt of his fear fully running out.

Her nubile, submissive pose:
Would be a precursor to those replicated, in his adulthood,
by the luxuriant oils of le Musée d'Orsay.

Knowing of the physical retaliation waiting,
he walked, once more, into that street:
His winter jacket's fur-lined collar, so comfy...

And then time came...
When all free will and choices had been expressed.

By men and things...
in one place... at one time.
A rich congruence of the first time... every time.

A slingshot… a roundish rock… a steady forearm.
Firm fingers on the handle. A pull on the rubber straps…
And… time is activated.

The "rock of justice"
for the "look of disrespect in the hallway"
flies through the air.

Direct hit on the collar, pushing his head to the right.
He should have been dead before hitting the ground.
The rock bounced off:

He was carrying a picture of his future in his book bag:
Three thousand miles away and ten years later.

A picture of Rockefeller Center:
Where he would look up, from the same angle, at the Chrysler building.

"Damn! I should have anticipated this curve!"
It had existed once in his past: Almost killing him:
It still existed again now… in front of his 68 VW.

The molecules of her parfum, fifty years later, still on his sweater.
As well as her knowing glances, next morning,
from across the 8'o'clock chemistry lab.

Making it… once again impossible to follow
any other road… crossing any other street.

And so… with vision of his imminent death against a tree:
… the front right tire remained on the road…

… And suddenly….
In the cold of a new England winter's night
The warmth…
No… the heat,
from the gentle touch of the palm of a hand on the back of his neck…

"Is that you Sidi Moussa?"
"Still keeping me safe?"

The humid breath of a lover.
The sweetly acrid taste of beads of sweat on her upper lips.

In the background the crash of tired waves:
All the way from the Labrador on this North African beach.
The Setting Sun... El Maghreb.
The greenish Atlantic.
Media beach: with its link to his future home:
This tiny American cemetery of G.I. who... will not... come home.

All of this world
within sight of what remains of their first kiss.

The kiss
that existed once and exists again
on the threshold of their adulthood.

When all was new and untouched.
Never to be the same or retraceable.

And yet... it happens again.
They are both young again.

The world... indeed does open like an oyster.
She reclines like the Olympia from the museum.

A magical mixture of youth and maturity:
of purposeful aggressive glance and birdlike febrility.

Moments written
into innocent wax, on a virginal slate.

A divine chance at second time,
in front of his teary mesmerized eyes.

"Seeing you once more...
would be knowing that I will lose you again."

But yet... ready to accept the darkest moments of existence:
the awareness of the ephemeral.

For a chance to touch once more
the ingots... of moments of soul-changing human passions...
smuggled out of Paradise... before the closing of the gates.

Paris: A Surrealist Dream

Epiphany of a nihilist:
Brando, "l'homme de l'absurde": *

Seeking salvation in the claustrophobic setting
of a stylish Saint Germain des prés apartment.

Quasi ritualistic mating of ethics and hedonism,
on impeccable grandeur of parquet floor…

Various degrees of pagan nudity.
Rustling sound of form-hugging Italian shirt.
Flashes of pink flesh among designer floral ensemble.

Urban altar offerings of intertwined bodies
to apparently pleased, voyeuristic gods.

Overwhelming, unverbalized excesses,
Among the silence of moralistic sanctions.

Celluloid world of sight… sounds and smells accented
—among the promiscuous touch—
by the presumed presence of sweet and sour organic acridity.

There is an ever-present Big-Bang, bassline sound in our temples:
a reminder, from our mortal soul,
of its losing fight against oblivion.

Like the privileged solar settings found on Grecian rocky islands,
there exist such times, places and persons,
when iconic messages, from iconic oracles, are proclaimed
to… the receptive souls,
to… the attuned artist,
messages, to the mesmerized listener.

About the disheartening, rock-hard realities
in wanting too much from our earthly allocated time.

Could this be in the nature of the enigmatic smirk:
full of disdain… soothing demonic visions… sleep-deprived stupor…
and yes…
child-like regret: In the slithering couple on the floor?

Revisiting the Jeanne and Paul personae in "Last tango in Paris."

* Comment heard about the similarity of the disabused attitude between Meursault and Brando (as Paul).

Organic Pieces... of That Kiss

In homage to the prehistoric "Venuses" and the latter Renoir paintings.

Elegant white-chalk, mathematical calculus arabesques:
Fitting dusty remnants of pure groundbreaking thought,
on a background of traditional blackboard, in leaky steam heat:
Febrile attempts by doctoral hopefuls,
to give... time and space... a human touch.

Knowing equations,
daring to capture flying pieces of the universe, inside the mass of inert mass:
Somewhere in the primordial soup...
a gem... the "God particle" awaits its reprise from the ceiling of the
Sistine chapel moment.

Like a mesmerizing gold ingot for a desert, thirst-crazed miner.
Like the lost-soul characters of *Waiting for Godot*.
Or the dedicated scientists, trying to simply find the mechanism.
If not the *Wizard's* purpose for Oz.

Thus, giving the orphaned human mind an illusionary drive:
that, somewhere, around the corner of a mathematical summation,
amidst a grouping of mind-numbing derivatives...
past last-ditch effort leaps at shortcut-assumptions.

Somehow getting past the frustration to equate both sides of the equation.
Finding kinship between relativity and quantum...

... untold light years, of practically empty space.
Connected bundles of energy and inert thought.
And still, no... *ON* switch!

All this thinking, using only our mind:
itself made of the very dust of this universe.
Thinking... from the inside...what is outside.

All this machinery... all these velocities... all this amperage.

While the poet... the artist...
thinks of the moment of *the kiss*.

This kiss…
now regressed into its untouchable… unreproducible past.

The scientist bends to science.
The poet does not.

The artist… ironically the confectioner of concretization:
by simply being, the dreamer
of *repeatable… ephemeral sighs.*

A lonely, driven, off-spring of Doctor Faust.
Yes! … that lovelorn fool!
Still working, in the poisonous mercury fumes of alchemy!

Simply wanting the miracle
of organic pieces of that kiss to crystalize on his lips.

The poet will patiently wait for science to catch up:
for the simultaneous closing of her eye lids,
and the imperceptible opening of her lips.

Rodin and Camille,
artists of the ephemeral and vaporous captured in marble,
must have felt the same thing, while rubbing one last time,
the contours of their respective statues.

Thus… artists… surely must have been going to their deaths…
knowing…
knowing that their words… those pearls from the piano keys,
the nuanced engorged shading of crimson skin-tones, from a half blind
Renoir…

that these artists must have had fleeting thoughts…
of the ultimate human heresy,
which is challenging the universe
into reversing time and space.

"Artists and their art, have, in their corner of the universe, been trying to travel though space and time without bothering with Einsteinian or Quantum theories." Comment expressed by a writer during a late night, Cognac induced conversation.

GLOSSARY

Alexis de Tocqueville: introduced to high school students as the visionary of the inherent democratic tendencies in the New World: ironically referred in the poem, in the light of the "coup d'état" nature of the American owners of Hawaiian plantation owners' action.

Algeria: see Albert Camus. (see Solinga, thesis) in this book the impact of the North African landscape on French writers. There is an oblique reference to the violence (witnessed by the author) of the colonial independence movement in "Tralfamadorian Man."

"Apocalypse Now": [see Viet Nam, see also "Full Metal Jacket"] In this book, it is, again and in particular, the nihilism of the Marlo Brando character in the violence of war.

Asymptote: a line that continually approaches a given curve but does not meet.

Baudelaire, Charles: his poems capture Paris (in particular: "Spleen de Paris") with an exceptional mix of realism, sensuality, and lyricism.

Beyle, Marie Henri (Stendhal): his novels are considered some of the earliest and finest nuanced (realistic) analyses of characters in love.

Bled: in Moroccan, the country-side (e.g. arid expanse: synonymous with "the sticks" in colloquial English).

(la) Bohème: associated with artistic (and dissipated) life in Paris of the later 19th century.

(la) Bonne Mère: in this book: the golden statue of the Virgin holding the Christ Child, protectively overlooking Marseille from granite hills.

Bosco, Jean and Henri: brothers associated with the presence of Morocco in French culture. Jean became a religious icon and Henri wrote some of the best early lyrical passages, both brothers having been heavily touched by the Maghreb. [see Solinga: thesis.]

Brandade (de morue): cod paste infused with olive oil and garlic. A day-long chore to make, before the advent of the food processor.

Camille, Claudel: exquisitely talented, but troubled sculptor, student and then intimate of Rodin. She became the equal of the master.

Casarès, Maria: talented actress; had a life-long, love affair with Albert Camus, which resulted in an important (and revealing) correspondence: The great philosopher falling in love in real-time.

Chemin du Roucas blanc: winding street going to the top of Marseille, where a boyhood friend of my mother's family was rounded up [in the last days of the war, after the landing of allied troops in Fréjus] with nine other men returning by tramway from work: Lined up and shot, as reprisal for a German soldier killed by the underground.

Corsica: the reference, in this book, is to the World War II years, during which the island was controlled by German Nazi and Italian Fascist troops, with consequences on the French families' access to food necessities.

Camus, Albert: in this book: The origin of the poems "On a cliff in North Africa" and "Meursault in love" as a result of a rereading of notes and biography of Albert Camus and thus my coming across a reference of the degradation of a memorial to the author over-looking Tipaza.

I refer the reader to the introduction to my dissertation, [University of Connecticut] which explains more fully my divorcing the realpolitik side of the Maghrebian setting from its purely physical impact, which states, in part: "It will be interesting to analyze the demarcation between the author and the narrator; and to what extent it is rendered fluid by the element of instantaneity of the glance."

[Il sera de même intéressant d'examiner comment l'espace écrivain/narrateur est affecté par l'effort observateur, c'est-à-dire comment l'effort `d'intégration' dans le site se reflète dans la forme. J'espère, comme résultat indirect à mon analyse, présenter les éléments qui existent dans cet `univers' qui appellent de nos jours la conscience occidentale. A quel niveau, par quels procédés imagiers voyons-nous aujourd'hui ce monde `différent' ? Y a-t-il quelque chose d'universel parmi certains aspects du topos du site maghrébin qui explique l'intérêt qui lui est encore accordé de nos jours? Quels sont les attributs particuliers de l'univers maghrébin qui se mettent en relief? Comment la pensée occidentale s'y cherche-t-elle ; comment s'y perd-t-elle? Comment le désert reflète-t-il et absorbe-t-il la présence humaine ? Quelle est l'évolution d'idées visionnaires à travers nos auteurs et leurs œuvres en question ? Comment chaque auteur a-t-il répondu aux forces esthétiques personnelles et externes pour éventuellement établir un rôle littéraire pour le paysage maghrébin ?]

Couscous: in the context of my poetry "Parisian couscous" is often a short-cut for cheap meals in le quartier Saint Michel in Paris; where French and Maghrebian cultures coexist.

Delacroix, Eugène: romantic painter known for his grandiose size and subject matter: [in particular in the Musée d'Orsay]

Disponible: Personal or ethical availability. [See Gide, Andre]

Febrile: having or showing a great deal of nervous excitement or energy.

"Flanders fields": see World War I. Ode to the famous poppies, which came to flourish thanks to or because of the churning effects of the bombardments.

"Full Metal Jacket": The sadistic behavior of the drill sergeant, in the movie, was of interest to me. It had been previously rationalized to me, in boot camp [at one-foot distance… "eye to eye"] as a necessary evil: "Private [with a note of sadness] … [insert my name] … I tried my best to toughen you for Viet Nam… I failed!"

German occupation: I tried to capture in the poem "Sea urchins," not the grand strategic view of war; but rather the parents' anguish in seeing hunger in their three or four-year-old children and the saving bounty of those sea urchins.

Gide, André: in his early "notebooks" and later major work on North Africa, "The Fruits of the Earth." Gide glorifies the pursuit of emotional and moral freedom from stifling societal norms in his concept of personal *disponibilité* or ethical availability. [see Solinga, thesis]

Hugo, Victor: unparalleled insertion of historical details in his novels, specifically, in his capture of the city of Paris. [les Misérables," "Notre Dame de Paris"]

Ionesco. Eugène: ("Le roi se meurt") In this avant-garde, absurdist play, Ionesco tries to capture the feeling of the "evaporation" or dissipation of Things from the point of view of the dying person (no matter how previously powerful). [the poem was inspired by a report of the fear, on the part of Stalin's staff, to approach his dying body].

"Je t'aime … moi non plus": iconic, non-sensical, nihilistic title of 1969, song by Serge Gainsbourg and Jane Birkin: "I love you… neither do I."

Joanna. Hiffernan: in this book, it is the symbolic intersection of this model in the respective, contrasting, and ultimately complementary visions [the carnal and angelic] by Gustave Courbet and James Whistler.

"Kid from the project": inspired by a real individual, whose biographical details, I purposely left out for creative freedom.

La bohème: dissipated life-style of the 19th century artists in Paris.

Le Clézio, Jean-Marie Gustave: in particular writer of "Désert," lyrical story based in the Maghreb. [see Solinga, thesis]

Loti, Pierre: one of the earliest French writers to glorify the imagery of the Maghreb. (see Solinga, thesis)

Last Tango in Paris: iconic sexually charged movie of the 1970's, by Bernando Bertolucci, with Marlon Brando and Maria Schneider.

Le roi se meurt: "Exit the king," absurdist play by Eugène Ionesco. The "act of dying," even from powerful persons, when, from the "protagonist's perspective" [the person dying] ... things and people (all the trappings of status) are symbolically disappearing.

The poem follows the process of a tyrant or brute with visions of his deeds, in this... a particularly unaccompanied trip... since, even the powerful cannot substitute one of the attendants to die in their stead.

Maquis: thick ground bush vegetation of the Southeastern part of France, used for camouflage by the Resistance during World War II. Hence, the name "Maquis" to mean the underground "Resistance."

Maghreb: Means "setting sun" in Arabic: the West [more particularly, the extreme Northwest of Africa (e.i. Morocco, Algeria, Tunisia).

Mehdia: Moroccan beach north of the Sidi Moussa of this book.

"Meursault in love": I had some hesitation about the title of this poem:

Camus is not Meursault. Meursault, the most iconic protagonists of the absurd! Meursault of *The Stranger* by Camus. But… my recalcitrance was vanquished upon reading [and rereading] the very intimate "Correspondence" of the philosopher that describe his falling in love in real time. These letters gave me a splendid… different insight from the university lectures who had somehow "canonized" … deified… the man/author/lover for me.

Miller, Henry: American writer whose sexually controversial books describes his life in 20th century Paris.

Montmartre: hill in Paris, crowned by the white-stone basilica of le Sacré Coeur. At the bottom of the hill, the "mount of martyrs," can be found the night-life of the Moulin Rouge.

Moses: central presence in my writing: pivotal "traveling companion" of the narrator in my "Sidi Moussa." [partially published]

Nuit de Chine: perfume created for Paul Poiret by perfumer Maurice Shaller. It has a sandalwood note suggesting incense from ancient China; the original bottle was said to suggest an opium bottle.

Orsay museum: former left bank train station: contains mostly 19th century works and in particular iconic romantic pieces.

Pastis: strong, anis-infused alcoholic apéritif.

Paul: in "Paris: Genesis of a muse" is the Marlo Brando character of *Last tango in Paris*. In keeping with the sexual anonymity of the relationship, their seems to be no last names in the movie script.

Poetic prose/ Lyrical prose/ Poèmes en prose: Baudelaire explored this hybrid world with the rich world of Paris in his "Spleen de Paris" and the "Flowers of evil." The flexibility of the genre was a perfect match for the urban setting of the city. Baudelaire's tortured soul and the complexity of this urban world have given us a quasi-magical language.

Pointe rouge: neighborhood on the eastern side of the Corniche of Marseille.

Queen Liliuokalani: Alexis de Tocqueville's name [associated with Democracy] is ironically referenced in the poem, since the queen was removed by a "coup d'état" promogulated by U. S. businessmen.

"Return from Viet Nam": The protagonist in this poem is fictionalized [what Marcel Proust would call a pastiche] from reality.

Rodin, Pierre August: in this book, it is his complicated, emotional relationship with the fragile and extremely talented Camille Claudel [his student] that is the focus of the poem.

Romanticism: latter 19th century powerful and painterly style and subject matter. [see Delacroix]

Rolla: character from an Alfred de Musset's poem of the same name. Jacques Rolla is a wealthy, but now bankrupted and debauched dandy, on the verge of suicide. He is described on his final night with the young courtesan Marie, whose very youth imparts virginal overtones in Rolla's glance.

Sacré Cœur: strikingly whitish-stone basilica on the hill of Montmartre, Paris.

Sahel: extensive arid, desertic region around and south of the Sahara. Le Clézio, Gide, Bosco, Loti (among others) have written breathless descriptions of the landscape.

Salé: Moroccan city [le Mellah, historic part] of Barbary coast fame. [across from the capital: Rabat] Location of the Mausoleum to Sidi Moussa [Marabout] and the "miniscule beach" mentioned in my writings.

Sidi Moussa: in Arabic, Lord Moses. The same prophet as in the Christian Old Testament and Koran. Traveling companion in my writing, who takes the narrator back from the "cold Labradorean present of the New World" to the "little beach" of youth and the rights of passage to sensuality. [the location of the "grotto" of the text.]

Serge Gainsbourg: composer of off-color and often sexually explicit lyrics of the 60's and 70's. [see: "je t'aime… moi non plus."]

Spahis: Cavalry unit of the late 19th and early 20th French army. Known for their splendid blue and red capes and endurance in the Maghrebian setting.

Stendhal: see "To the happy few."

"The sublime versus the grotesque": Victor Hugo's iconic phrase describing his view describing the contrasting sides of man's nature and behavior.

"To the happy few": (see Stendhal ["Le rouge et le noir," "The Charterhouse of Parma"] Stendhal's book dedications "To the happy few," referred to the few people who would truly understand his writing. It could be a reference to Lord Byron's "Don Juan."

"Tragedy, Despair and Hope": the subject of this poem: the real death of workers of a dam break, would have necessitated scrupulous factual research and respectful privacy for the families. I opted, instead, once again, for a lyrical filter: Which honors the survivors and allows the freedom of poetic license.

Verlaine, Paul: French romantic-era poet. Unabashed sensitive views of Paris. Such as: "Il pleure dans mon cœur/ Comme il pleut sur la ville" [It is crying in my heart/ As it is raining over the city].

Viel, Simone: Shoah survivor, who bravely took up human rights and in particular, women-rights issues, as a French politician.

Viet Nam: [see "Kid From the Project"] A half century later (1969-2018) [date of the writing of "Kid from the project" poem], I was surprised how close to the surface the scars of this era were still hiding in my soul: Racism, the boot camp de-sensitization of recruits, loss of ethical references… (See also: "Full metal jacket.").

Vonnegut, Kurt: of interest in this book, is the "flexible, non-linear concept of time (in "Slaughter House Five," in particular.) The poem refers, in part, to "reliving" a near fatal assault prevented by a "fur collar."

"We'll always have Paris.": iconic line by disabused Humphrey Bogart's character in the Classic film, "Casablanca."

Whistler, James: see Joanna Hifferman

World War I: was unfortunately a fertile topic for poets: "Le dormeur du val," by Arthur Rimbaud and "Flanders Fields" by John McCrae capture the intimate, emotional toll.

Yves Montand: French singer of iconic songs capturing the romance of Paris: particularly: "À Paris" … "Sous le ciel de Paris." Or "l'âme des poètes," by Charles Trénet.

INDEX

Titles in bold and first lines in italics.

ABOUT THE AUTHOR

Jean-Yves Vincent Solinga

Jean-Yves' family comes from Provence. He was born in Algeria, and lived thereafter between the south of France and Morocco in what he describes as an idyllic youth. Upon settling in America with his family, at the age of 15, he had already been writing poetry: being first published in "A Letter Among Friends" along with John Norman of New London, CT. After serving in the U.S. Army, he began a successful career in teaching and lecturing. Jean-Yves holds a doctorate in French on the representation of the Maghrebian [North African] landscape found in the texts by Pierre Loti, André Gide, Albert Camus and Jean-Marie Le Clézio. He has published several books of poetry: *Clair-Obscur of the Soul* (2008), *Clair-obscur de l'âme* [in French] (2008), *In the Shade of a Flower* (2009), *Landscape of Envies* (2010), *Words Made of Silk* (2011), *Impressions of Reality* (2013),

Artist in a Pixelated World (2014), *Asymptotes at the Limit of Passion* (2015), and *Created Realities* (2017).

In *Paris: Genesis of a Muse,* continuing to use an infrastructure of poetic prose, Jean-Yves aims for a linguistic landscape that lives between hard reality and vaporous passion: exploring the contrasting worlds of the euphoria of sensual happiness and the inevitability of its end.

Many of his poems have a personal as well as societal breath. It is often a singularly unique view of mankind's reflection through the prism of the lyrical language with, at times an impressionistic poetry, tackling many hard realities of history and society.

The author has been a featured speaker at the Alliance Française of New Haven and Hartford; Presented on the theme of Le déracinnement (Cultural uprooting) at the International Colloquium: 20th- / 21st- Century French Studies at the University of Connecticut, the Center of the Teaching of French at Yale; The University and Southern Connecticut State University on the use of poetry in language studies; Published in *Art et poésie* edited by the renowned French poet Jean-Claude George. He has also read at the Poetry Institute of New Haven; Wesleyan University book store; the Cantab Lounge in Cambridge, the Blue Star Café in Providence, the Guilford Green Barn. He has featured at the Arts café in Mystic; the Hygienic; the Bean and leaf; the Bank Square Bookstore. He has co-featured at the Mystic Art Gallery, and at the Harriet Beecher Stowe Center on the theme of social justice in poetry. Jean-Yves has had poems published by the *Free Poet Collective Ekpharsis Project* at the New Britain museum, the *Ekpharsis Loft Anthology of Providence* and the *Little Red Tree Anthology,* the *Exquisite Project of the Bill Libraries*; as well as several poems published in *The Peacock Journal.* His poetry has been nominated three times for a Pushcart Award.

Jean-Yves Solinga is a poet of immense ability and range whose lyricism is truly remarkable. It contains many breathtakingly beautiful and sophisticated poems that reach out to the very limits of the human condition where true art exists. Many facets of his work continue to find inspiration and perspective in his cultural duality.

Photograph by Elaine Solinga

www.ingramcontent.com/pod-product-compliance
Lightning Source LLC
Chambersburg PA
CBHW050354100426

42739CB00015BB/3395